"We hav

and he

Pondering Pogo's Enemy

One Opinion Piece at a time

By Herb Van Fleet

* The quote "We have met the enemy, and they are us" is from a comic strip called "Pogo," created by Walt Kelly in the 1940's, featuring a possum named "Pogo." The statement was actually a twist on Admiral Oliver Perry's words after a naval battle: "We have met the enemy, and they are ours." The updated version was first used by Walt Kelly in the 1960s and referred to the turmoil caused by the Vietnam War.

Editing and Formatting: Jamie Birdwell-Branson

Cover Graphics: Inspired Cover Designs

Publisher: PPE Publishing

ISBN: 978-1-5323-1760-6

Dedication:

This book is dedicated to Carol Stark, Managing Editor of the Joplin Globe in Joplin, Missouri. Without her support and encouragement I would never have written or had published my Op-Eds over the years. And no Op-Eds, no book!

Acknowledgment:

To my daughter Toby who suggested the book in the first place and then helped with its organization. She also provided ideas for alternate distribution methods. Of course, she continued her support for this project and gave me much needed encouragement throughout the publishing process.

Special Thanks:

I appreciate the help of David Pharris and Huiwen Helen Zhang in helping with the cover design of this book. And for their friendship.

TABLE OF PONDERINGS

PREFACE

A few years ago, I decided to write a book, but I didn't have anything in mind to write about. I was interested in current events so my first tentative entry into writing was through letters-to-the-editor. Many of these were published in the local paper, The Tulsa World in Tulsa, Oklahoma. But I also submitted LTEs to my hometown paper, The Joplin Globe in Joplin, Missouri. However, several of those I sent to the Globe were somewhat lengthy and more than the typical 250-300 words most newspapers allow.

At some point, the Globe made my lengthy LTEs into op- eds and gave me credit as a "Guest Columnist." Thereafter, I contributed more and more columns.

Eventually, the "guest" went away, and the paper, for whatever reason, decided I was to be designated "Columnist." As of July 21, 2016, I have had 50 columns published in the Joplin Globe.

Given that volume of material, it looked like I had in effect written a book. The question then became one of selecting which op-eds to include. After making the selections, I found they could be divided into five categories:

- Economic Issues
- Governance and Democracy
- National Security
- Political Issues
- Social Issues

Regardless of the category, each of the op-eds here is my reflection on certain aspects of our social institutions and culture.

But the opinions, of course, came from my own worldview as applied to what I was seeing in the world around me.

As the writing progressed, and with the subject matter sometimes bordering on the absurd, I often thought of the famous Pogo declaration, "We have met the enemy and he is us." Then the wheels started turning in my meager brain.

My pondering, contemplating, mulling, and cogitating about the human condition and expressing the same through a series of op-ed's seemed to make sense. So, in keeping with this overall theme, I titled this book, "Pondering Pogo's Enemy."

I have selected some of what I think are the more interesting, diverse, and sometimes controversial of my commentaries to include here. Some of these appear as they were originally published. A number of others were expanded and revised as I had time. I also added a few quotations pertinent to the topic that were not in the original piece to underscore and emphasize my point.

I added some references too as needed to identify the sources for the material that were not published due to restrictions on the word-count permitted by the Globe.

Of course, most of the commentary here is time-dependent and things will have likely changed by the time this book is read. There are statistics, for example, that were current at the time of the writing, but have not been updated.

Nonetheless, I hope the reader can just enjoy seeing another point of view. I hope, too, that these writings may provide ideas for essays, or for research, or even for use in an op-ed. In any case, I hope you enjoy reading these opinions as much as I enjoyed writing them.

ECONOMIC ISSUES

1.1   Blaming Henry Ford

September 23, 2011

I blame Henry Ford. Everybody's blaming somebody for all the messes we're in these days. So, I blame Henry Ford.

Ford's introduction of the affordable Model T in 1908, which was manufactured using an "assembly line," became the springboard for numerous other industries that, with a few hiccups along the way, have produced the greatest economic expansion and prosperity the world has ever seen.

The oil industry boomed along with the steel industry and many others related to the manufacture of automobiles. Road construction also took off so that all those horseless carriages could get around much easier. Our mostly agrarian economy became mostly industrial as many left their farms to seek their fortune in other parts of the country.

During the Great Depression, many of President Roosevelt's programs helped to create a vast infrastructure built around the automobile. And that, with some help from the GI Bill after World War II, put millions of Americans on the road to suburbia.

Home ownership then became the asset of choice. This spurred a concomitant growth in the home construction industry as well as in the home furnishings, fixtures and appliance manufacturers, along with the utility companies and the home supply and home repair industries.

Financial institutions also saw phenomenal growth during this period — banks, savings and loans, credit unions and insurance companies. But, the automobile still held sway. In the 1950s the mantra was, "What's good for General Motors is good for the country." Much of this would have been more difficult, I argue, without Henry Ford and his Model T.

But, there's more. To keep labor unions at bay, and to reduce employee turnover, Ford stunned the industry with his $5 per day plan in 1914, which almost doubled the average worker's pay of $3 per day. Later he would offer a profit-sharing plan, but only to those who were qualified by his "social department." Of course, Ford was not about altruism. He was about the money.

For those manufacturers that refused to follow Ford's lead in the treatment of employees, labor unions stepped in to fight for benefits. As a result, collective bargaining units became a significant part of the work force in virtually all industries, peaking in 1954 with 28.3% of all employees. (See CRS Report to Congress, "Union Membership Trends in the United States," August 31, 2004.)

During the first half of the 20th century, the notions of outsourcing and downsizing were unheard of. Unions were therefore able to obtain substantial benefits for their members during this period, including paid vacation and sick leave, health insurance and retirement/pension programs. But, as productivity increased and as cheap labor became available elsewhere in the world, union membership declined along with America's manufacturing base. According to the report cited above, in 2003, unions comprised only 11.5% of the labor force. But, the legacy of their fight for employee benefits still lingers. After all, who wants to give up weekends?

Also, during the 1950s and 1960s, Japan and Germany had mostly recovered from World War II and had established a substantial manufacturing base that was very competitive with the

U.S., including automobile brands like Toyota and Volkswagen, and electronics — lots of electronics. But, while Americans were trying to set the clocks on their VHS players, India, and later China, decided they would rather establish their own industrial base. In fact, during the 1980s with the introduction of the personal computer, information technology would overtake manufacturing as the new growth industry; much of it coming from Asia.

Somewhere along the way the idea of "globalization" entered the vocabulary. White collar and blue-collar workers alike were left to the mercy of their employers. Strikes by unions were no longer effective against low-cost labor in other parts of the world. As a result "at-will" employees became expendable. As corporate America unburdened itself from the expense of its workers and sought cheap labor elsewhere, the middle class eroded and the disparity between the haves and have-nots in income and wealth grew further apart. It was then left to government and to the rest of society to provide some kind of safety net for the dispossessed.

All the presidents and members of Congress since the Great Depression have expanded government involvement into virtually every aspect of our lives. The Social Security system was expanded to include virtually all workers, their spouses and children, and even added disability benefits

And don't forget Medicare and Medicaid. To help the poor, the government offers welfare payments, food stamps, minimum wages and unemployment benefits. Then there is government help for homeowners with government-backed mortgages, for college students with grants, for farmers with subsidies for crops and, for all of us, more security (some say) with the largest military in the world. Meanwhile, the cost of all this benevolence began to add up.

As a result of all this tinkering, everybody now has a stake in government. Consequently, special interest groups sprang up and Washington has become overrun with lobbyists. Of course, the elected officials tend to pay more attention to those with deep pockets since election campaigns are expensive. So, the rich are rewarded the most, not only by pork-barrel projects, but through the tax code, which, according to President Obama's Economic Recovery Advisory Board, has been changed 15,000 times since 1986. All this favoritism, all the promises made, have come at great cost. And we've been painfully reminded of that in the recent "debt ceiling" debate. Congress has been sawing on the wrong side of the limb for a long time. But hey, that's what we voted for.

So, I lay all this at the feet of the late Henry Ford with his Model T moving lazily down the assembly line. His vision helped propel the idea that we could have it all, that we could have it all now, and that we could do it all on the cheap. On the other hand, as Ford himself once said:

"Don't find fault, find a remedy; anybody can complain."

1.2   Minimum Wage and Big Business

December 16, 2013

During the recent Thanksgiving holiday, it was a little depressing to see workers picketing Walmart stores in cities around the country complaining of unfair work hours and low wages.

Walmart, with 1.4 million employees, is the largest private employer in the U.S., making it a bellwether for other employers who rely on minimum and below-minimum wage employees, including other retailers, restaurants, hotels/motels, and the like.

There is no mystery here as to Wal-Mart's motive for keeping wages low — profit maximization. After all, employee compensation is a significant cost for most companies. So lower employee cost means higher profits and more cash for stockholders.

Indeed, profit maximization is the objective for most business establishments. And that objective is being met by most of them. The Commerce Department's Bureau of Economic Analysis reports that after-tax corporate profits have increased 271 percent since the fourth quarter of 2008. In fact, those profits have reached record highs in four of the last five years.

Meanwhile, the federal minimum hourly wage of $7.25 has not changed since 2009. It's no wonder, then, that minimum wage earners, especially those with children, need public assistance. And public assistance comes largely from taxpayers — you and me.

Speaking of which, a congressional report released last May provides an estimate of the dollar value of welfare programs provided to Wal-Mart's work force. According to an article in The Huffington Post dated May 31, 2013, a single 300-person Walmart Supercenter store in Wisconsin likely costs taxpayers more than

$1.7 million per year for Medicaid, food stamps, WIC (Supplemental Nutrition Program for Women, Infants and Children, and other federal aid. That comes out to about $5,800 per Walmart employee—and that's just for one store!

Now multiply Wal-Mart's 1.4 million employees by $5,800 per worker and the total is almost $8.2 billion annually that we taxpayers are, in effect, subsidizing that company. That $5,800 also means taxpayers add about $2.79 per hour per employee for government assistance programs, bringing the minimum up to $10.04. In other words, taxpayers provide 28 percent of benefits to employees not covered by Walmart.

Of course, the minimum wage concept has had its critics since it was adopted in 1937. For example, the conservative economist Milton Friedman declared: "The consequences of minimum wage laws have been almost wholly bad. ... In my opinion there is absolutely no positive objective achieved by minimum wages." And Ronald Reagan piped in with, "The minimum wage has caused more misery and unemployment than anything since the Great Depression." In 2004, David Brandon, the CEO of Domino's Pizza, announced: "From our perspective, raising the minimum wage is a 'job killer,'" a phrase often repeated by House Speaker John Boehner and other conservatives.

But such criticism is pure hogwash. None of the fears about the dire consequences of the minimum wage have come to pass. I submit that their comments are only meant to assuage concerns of the big business contributors to political campaigns, mostly Republicans, and make assurances that wages are not going up on their watch.

In point of fact, raising the minimum wage is good for business and the overall economy. Why? Because when poor workers have more money to spend, they spend it, almost entirely in the local community, on basic necessities like housing, food, clothing and transportation. When consumer demand grows, businesses thrive, earn more profits, and create more jobs. Economists call this the "multiplier effect."

To underscore that point, a March 13 study from the Economic Policy Institute shows that a hike in the minimum wage to the Senate-proposed $10.10 by 2015 would affect 30 million workers, increase their wages by $51.5 billion and add 140,000 net new jobs to the economy.

About 100 years ago, Henry Ford increased the wages of his factory workers from the going rate of $3 per day to $5. He did so to make sure his employees could afford the Model T Fords they were producing. That sizable increase in wages promoted morale, reduced employee turnover and the associated training costs, kept labor unions at bay, and expanded the markets for Ford Motor Co., which more than offset the increase in wages.

But these days businesses with minimum or below minimum wage workers can afford the employee turnover and training costs without much sacrifice in profits.

Unemployment now being what it is, hiring is not a problem. Besides, they don't have to worry about their employees' financial stress. We taxpayers will help to take care of that.

Now if we could just get Walmart to put us on its profit-sharing plan.

1.3   The Tragedy of Self-Interest

March 1, 2015

"It is not from the benevolence of the butcher, the brewer, or the baker, that we expect our dinner, but from their regard to their own interest. We address ourselves, not to their humanity but to their self- love, and never talk to them of our necessities but of their advantages."—Adam Smith

Back in the dark ages of 1968, an ecologist by the name of Garret Hardin wrote a piece for the journal "Science" called "The Tragedy of the Commons." The idea Hardin presents is relatively simple: individuals acting independently and rationally according to their own economic self-interest can behave contrary to the best interests of the whole group by taking advantage of common resources.

Dr. Hardin's essay expands on the Malthusian theory that when a population increases at a rate faster than its means of subsistence, then, unless the growth rate is checked by moral restraint or by disease, famine, war or other disaster, widespread poverty and social degradation will inevitably result. Such effects are the consequence of an unsustainable consumption of resources.

Consider, for example, the events on St. Andrews Island in the Bering Sea. In August 1944, the U.S. Coast Guard established a small base there. As a backup food supply, they had 29 reindeer shipped to the island. The animals landed in an ungulate paradise: lichen mats four inches thick carpeted large areas of the island. The only predators were the men on the island, and they left at the end of the war without having killed any of the reindeer, leaving them to fend for themselves. In 1957, Dave Klein, a biologist working for the U.S. Fish and Wildlife Service, visited the island. At that time Klein counted 1,350 very fat and happy reindeer. But the dark shadow of Malthus was looming large. Klein returned in 1963 and estimated there were 6,000 in the herd.

When Klein returned in the summer of 1966, he, another biologist and a botanist found the island covered with skeletons; they counted only 42 live reindeer. There were no fawns and only one sickly looking male. Shortly thereafter, the 32-mile long, four-mile wide island of St. Matthew was barren of reindeer.

But reindeer are migratory animals and can travel more than 3,000 miles per year. Being trapped on an island that offered no more than 1 percent of that distance, their limited resources were unable to be replenished in the face of a growing population. Then, too, they lacked the planning skills of we humans.

As a way of avoiding such disasters due to overpopulation, Hardin argues that if families were solely dependent on their own resources for survival so that those families that were less respectful of the environment would see their own children starve, overbreeding would be corrected by nature and there would be no need for the welfare state.

As to the tragedy of the commons involving humans, Dr. Hardin uses the example of herders sharing a common parcel of land on which they are each entitled to let their cows graze. In England, shepherds sometimes grazed their sheep in such common areas. But the sheep ate more grass than the cows. If a shepherd added more sheep in his self-interest to get more economic benefits, then overgrazing results and the common could be depleted or even destroyed to the detriment of all; i.e., the tragedy.

This is an example of the tension between individuals and their particular group with respect to a limited but common resource available to all. Under such conditions, as the individual tries to gain an advantage for his or her self-interest, the interest of the whole group suffers.

But even the private ownership of property, which would allow for management and maintenance of the resource, does not solve the problem.

For instance, the Grand Banks off the coast of Newfoundland was once regarded as home to an endless supply of cod. In the 1960s and 1970s, advances in fishing technology allowed huge catches of cod. As a result, the fish populations dropped and by the 1990s, cod populations were so low that the Grand Banks fishing industry collapsed. It was too late for regulation and management; the cod stocks had been irreparably damaged. Since then, the cod populations have remained low, and some scientists doubt the Grand Banks ecosystem will ever recover.

Then there is the drought in California and the availability of water from aquifers. These underground water sources are mostly used by farmers for irrigating crops. But when the farmers upstream of the aquifer take too much water, leaving those down-stream with too little, the end result is a reduction of this resource for many farmers and thus a drop in the food supply for all, along with an increase in cost.

The consequences of Hardin's theory can also been seen in our capitalistic economy — where self-interest flourishes. The stock market crash of 1929 and the resulting Great Depression, the Savings and Loan debacle in the 1980s, the "Dot-Com" bubble in the late 90s, and the "housing" bubble that lead to the current Great Recession in 2008, are all examples of individuals and businesses pursing their own self-interest, aided and abetted by banks and brokers, until it blew up in their faces and, in so doing, brought down many millions who were just minding their own business.

These days, for-profit corporations pledge their allegiance more to stockholders than stakeholders, especially labor, financial capital over human capital. High unemployment rates allow businesses to keep wages low, sometimes to the point where underpaid employees need government-funded welfare to make ends meet. And welfare comes from taxpayers, which, in effect, subsidizes companies' profits.

The tragedy here is the decline of labor income, which forms the aggregate demand for goods and services — the primary resource that drives the economy. There will be more bubbles that burst and more stock market gyrations. There will be more technology to replace workers and more globalization to save even more labor costs. And the consequences affect us all. Such is the nature of the capitalist commons.

Garret Hardin's "tragedy" also implies elements involving morality, responsibility, fairness, duty, cooperation and mutual respect as offsets to mitigate self-interest, which is not for an egalitarian society, but for a sustainable one. We ignore those important values at our own peril.

After all, "commons" include air, water, biota and public land shared by everyone. And the tragedy of these commons is already happening. Global warming is a threat to our food supply, to the availability of potable water and to the disastrous consequences of rising ocean levels.

And, sustainability is becoming more critical as resources are consumed faster than they can be replaced and/or replenished. Increasing populations are pushing the plant to its very limits.

In fact, resource consumption in the United States is so great that it takes an estimated four earths to maintain that level. And much of that demand has to do with satisfying the goal of increasing economic growth where the resource is fiscal — not physical.

The driver of the rush, then, to accumulate wealth is via capitalism. But, as noted above, the priorities of commercial enterprises do not include, or rarely include, consideration of the commons. It is the short-term, self-interest pursuit of profits over the long-term consequences.

One possible answer to this dilemma may be found in the Haudenosaunee's (Iroquois Confederacy) Great Law of Peace. (See Op-Ed 2.1 - "Planning Seven Generations Ahead.")

Of course, planning seven generations ahead (140 years or so is anathema in a capitalist society where the planning only extends to the next quarterly dividend payment. That said, there is a small, 92-page book available, "Our Responsibility to the Seventh Generation," that discusses this concept in more detail. The authors offer this in explaining their philosophy of sustainability (pp. 74-75:)

"Sustainability for traditional Indigenous Peoples means ensuring the survival of the people, the land and the resources for seven generations. Because of their understanding of the need to respect the earth, Indigenous people have much to offer to the identification of sustainable development strategies. The survival of the planet has been compromised by practices based upon the belief, that the earth has an unlimited capacity to absorb pollutants that the land can be modified and manipulated to change or to increase the carrying capacity of the land. The unequal distribution of the resource, which has historical roots, has resulted in the depletion of resources in certain areas. It is these practices that have arisen from the attitude that is responsible for the damage to the planet's support systems. The earth's destruction is the result of societies having lost a sense of the earth's sacredness."

But of course, we as a society have failed to follow the wisdom of the Haudenosaunee, which was known long before the Industrial Revolution and the rise of capitalism.

As a result of the mismanagement and irresponsibility regarding our limited natural resources, we are like the reindeer on St. Andrews Island. The population is increasing, the business world is thriving, and the earth is dying.

1.4 Drug Companies and Free Enterprise

November 29, 2015

By now, I suppose almost everybody has heard about the guy who raised the price of Daraprim—a drug used in the treatment of AIDS and some cancers— to $750.00 from $13.50. The guy is Martin Shkreli, a former hedge fund manager, who used his fortune to form a company called Turing Pharmaceuticals, which acquired the rights to Daraprim. The 5,500 percent increase in price became headline news and Shkreli quickly became the most hated man on earth," surpassing even the dentist who killed Cecil the Lion.

Although Shkreli promised to lower the price of Daraprim, he has not done so as of this writing. In an October 9, 2015, post on "Business Insider," Lydia Ramsey reports that with the wholesale cost, along with specific pharmacy fees, "a 30-day, 30- pill supply of Daraprim would cost me $27,006 at my local pharmacy." That comes out to $900 a pill. According to an October 12, 2015, article on Reuters.com the same medicine is sold in Britain by GlaxoSmithKline for 66 cents!

Daraprim is not the only drug priced through the strato- sphere. Last August, Rodelis Therapeutics acquired the rights to Cycloserine, a tuberculosis drug, from the Purdue Research Foundation. Rodelis then jumped the price from $500 for 30 capsules to $10,800. After a highly critical article of Rodelis by the New York Times, the drug was transferred back to PRF, which then dropped the price to $1,050, which is still a doubling of price—and for no apparent reason.

Some lawmakers and a few presidential candidates have expressed their outrage over these price increases and the cost of other pharmaceuticals that have doubled, tripled, or gone up even more within the last few years.

On November 4, 2015, a bipartisan committee in the Senate, co-chaired by Susan Collins (R-Maine) and Missouri's Clair Mc-Caskill (D-Mo), was formed to begin an investigation into pharmaceutical drug pricing, including the pricing of older and off-patent drugs that were made after company acquisitions or mergers.

This is all well and good, but probably for naught. Open-Secrets.Org, states that, in 2014, the pharmaceutical and health industries spent over $230 million for lobbying. And from 1998 through 2012, they spent $2.6 billion on those activities, more than any other industry.

And these investments have paid off. The Medicare Prescription Drug bill, known as Part D, was written by Big Pharma. Among other things, the bill prohibits Medicare from negotiating drug prices. The Veterans Administration, on the other hand, can and does negotiate drug prices.

The industry also got its way in the Affordable Care Act (Obamacare), which provides that a drug can only be purchased from private industry, not from government or non-profit sources.

Of course, the biggest boon to Big Pharma is the Prescription Drug Marketing Act of 1987. This law makes it illegal for anyone other than the original manufacturer to bring prescription drugs into this country. That is, Americans are prohibited from buying cheaper drugs from Canada, Europe, or any other countries.

To wit: in 2013, a 30 day supply of the drug Abilify costs $199.70 from an online Canadian drugstore, but $711.83, if ordered at Walgreens, that according to an article from ElderLaw Answers, "Buying Prescription Drugs From Canada: Legal or Illegal? And the New York Times reports in its article "The Soaring Cost of a Simple Breath," that the prescription nasal spray Rhinocort Aqua was selling for more than $250 a month in Oakland pharmacies that year but cost less than $7 in Europe, where it is available over the counter.

Then there are the patents on new drugs. That gives the pharmaceutical manufacturers a 20-year monopoly, thereby prohibiting competition and allowing them to set whatever price they believe the market will bear.

In spite of this monopoly power, drug companies still advertise. According to the Pew Charitable Trusts, in 2012, Big Pharma spent more than $24 billion on marketing to physicians, and over $3 billion on advertising (mainly through television commercials. The United States and New Zealand are the only developed nations that allow drug companies to advertise prescription drugs directly to the public.

At the end of the day, with their influence on Congress, with favorable legislation, and with patent protection, the drug companies have managed to cut off Adam Smith's invisible hand of consumer choice. In other words, there is virtually no free market for American purchasers of prescribed pharmaceuticals.

To add insult to injury, the extraordinary and often unjustified high price of drugs means that many prescriptions will go unfilled, or that some patients will be forced into bankruptcy, or both.

Now we have the mega-merger of Pfizer and Allegan worth about $155 billion, making it the world's biggest drug maker. The new company will headquarter in Ireland to lower its tax burden. Surely, it will then pass those savings on through lower drug prices. Surely it will.

GOVERNANCE AND DEMOCRACY

2.1 Planning Seven Generations Ahead

October 31, 2011

This country has come to feel the same when Congress is in session as when the baby gets hold of a hammer."—Will Rogers

---

A recent poll shows the approval rating of Congress at a miserable and embarrassing 8.0 percent. This, together with recent demonstrations from the Tea Party folks and the Occupy (fill in the blank) groups, exemplify a growing discontent with the direction this country is headed. Indeed, there are many challenges to be dealt now and over the next few years that will impact not only our political and our economic systems, but most of our social institutions as well.

From what I'm seeing, it is not beyond reason to assume that the United States is about to come off the rails and that we are at serious risk of losing our viability as a nation.

Given this predicament, perhaps our form of government as practiced here in the early part of the 21st century is due, even overdue, for a time-out.

But not to worry. There is an alternative and it's waiting in our own back yard. (Well, actually in upstate New York.) It is the League of the "Haudenosaunee," which means the "People of the Longhouse." Originally, this League of Indian tribes consisted of the Mohawks, Oneidas, Onondagas, Cayugas, and Senecas, so it was called "The Five Nations" by the British. (Later, the Tuscarora joined, making it the Six Nations.) But the League is better known by its French name, "Iroquois." And its government is called the "Iroquois Confederacy."

This political system was conceived by a Huron prophet called "Peacemaker," whose vision of a unified nation became the "Great Law of Peace." But it was put into practice by the Onondaga chief Hiawatha, who became famous through Henry Wadsworth Longfellow's poem "The Song of Hiawatha,"

It is uncertain when the confederacy first came into being. Some scholars believe it could have been as early as 1090 or 1150 CE. If those dates are accurate, then the Great Law of Peace preceded even the Magna Carta, "The Great Writ," of 1215 CE, which became the foundation for English Law and the inspiration for many Constitutions, including ours.

Although there are too many aspects of the Iroquois Confederacy's political philosophy to go into here, a few are worth noting.

First and foremost, and for you women's libbers out there, much of the political power of the confederacy was in the hands of the elder women. They could veto treaties or declarations of war, they appointed members of their clan to the Grand Council, and if any member failed to comply with the wishes of the women of his tribe and the Great Law, the mother could demote him. Iroquois women could also own and sell property and do so without the permission of any patriarch. This gender equality would later become an inspiration to Elizabeth Cady Stanton, Lucretia Mott, and others in the Women's Suffrage movement.

The members of the Grand Council, as well as the military leaders, accepted no salary, and gave away any perquisites they might have received. There was no bribery or corruption in office; they felt amply rewarded by the confidence and esteem of the people. In fact, the motivating ethic here was honor and trust. And the punishment for those who misbehaved was shame and dishonor, which, to the guilty, was much worse than a prison sentence.

Of particular significance today is this section of the Great Law:

"Whenever a specially important matter or a great emergency is presented before the Confederate Council and the nature of the matter affects the entire body of the Five Nations, threatening their utter ruin, then the Lords of the Confederacy must submit the matter to the decision of their people and the decision of the people shall affect the decision of the Council. This decision shall be a confirmation of the voice of the people."

Here is democracy in action—seven hundred years before ours! With regard to "the coming generations," Oren Lyons Chief of the Onondaga Nation, writes:

"In all of your deliberations in the Council, in your efforts at law making, in all your official acts, self-interest shall be cast into oblivion. . . Look and listen for the welfare of the whole people and have always in view not only the present but also the coming generations, even those whose faces are yet beneath the surface of the ground - the unborn of the future Nation."

"We are looking ahead, as is one of the first mandates given us as chiefs, to make sure and to make every decision that we make relate to the welfare and well-being of the seventh generation to come. . . . What about the seventh generation? Where are you taking them? What will they have?"

Planning for seven generations? How about putting that requirement on Congress?

The Great Law of Peace also had a measurable impact on our Constitution. This fact was acknowledged by the 100th Congress in 1988, via House Consent Resolution 331, which states in pertinent part,

" . . . the confederation of the original Thirteen Colonies into one republic was influenced by the political system developed by the Iroquois Confederacy as were many of the democratic principles which were incorporated into the Constitution itself."

Testament to this influence occurred during the 1787 Constitutional Convention, when John Rutledge of South Carolina read some tracts from the Great Law, one of which echoes the Preamble to our Constitution:

"We, the people, to form a union, to establish peace, equity, and order . . ."

So, what we have here is a proven system of governance, one that promotes egalitarianism, and one that incorporated the philosophies of Locke, Montesquieu, Hume, and Rousseau hundreds of years before those political philosophers were born. And it has lasted almost one thousand years! Compare the Iroquois Confederacy with the dystopia that plagues us today. Seems to me like an alternative worth considering.

We just need to get the hammer away from the baby.

2.2   What is the Power of We The People?

January 10, 2012

"The Constitution only gives people the right to pursue happiness. You have to catch it yourself."—Benjamin Franklin

---

The Joplin Globe's editorial "People Power" (Dec. 28, 2011), touched on a number of issues that have bothered me for some time. Although I'm neither a Constitutional lawyer nor scholar, I have researched some of the questions raised there as well as many others that have concerned me over the years.

First, you might be surprised to learn that the three words that begin the Preamble of our Constitution, "We the People," are misleading at best, and untrue at worst. That's because the people didn't and never have ratified this foundational document of our government. That was done by the legislatures of the original 13 states. Even the amendments, including the Bill of Rights, were not voted on by the people, but, again, by the state legislatures.

Of course back in the day, the "We" in "We the people," were, in truth, an elitist class that did not include women, African-Americans, Native Americans or the poor—among many other groups. Our founders were the equivalent of European aristocracy in the 18th century. Not much has changed in the last 200 years—we still have an elitist class running the country; although, admittedly, a more inclusive one.

There were 55 delegates to the Constitutional Convention in 1787, representing all the states but Rhode Island. Each delegate was selected by his respective state legislature, and was not, again, elected by the people. When it was all said as done, 39 delegates signed the new Constitution; a little over two-thirds majority, The Convention adjourned on September 17, which became known as Constitution Day. But each year that date goes virtually unnoticed. We the people celebrate our independence, not our form of government.

From its Latin roots, the term democracy means "people rule." But under our form of government, the people's involvement in democracy at the federal level is very limited. We can vote for only one out of the 435 Representatives in Congress and two out of the 100 in the Senate. (Up until 1913,

U.S. senators were appointed, not elected.) We don't even directly vote for president; we vote for "electors." But even here, the electors in most states use the "winner take all" rule, which means that the votes for the runners-up don't even count. But thanks for showing up anyway.

Further, those of us registered as Independent — 24 million and growing according to USA Today — can't vote in the primaries in most states, or have delegates to the presidential conventions. We're stuck with having to choose between candidates selected for us without having a voice in the process. As more and more defectors from the political parties join the ranks of the unaffiliated, what little democracy we can cling to becomes more and more diminished.

So what we have, technically, is a Constitutional Republic, not a Democratic Republic. We the people were never given the power to establish our government in the first place, and we are extremely limited in selecting and then voting for people to run it for us. And how is that working out? Well, recent polls say that something north of 70 percent of us think that the country is headed in the wrong direction, that over 90 percent of us think Congress is doing a bad job, and that more than half of us disapprove of the work of the Obama administration and the Supreme Court.

A good part of the reason for this difficulty, in my view, is that the framers grossly underestimated the influence of what they called "factions." These groups would include out-spoken dissenters including members of the political parties themselves, along with the Tea Partiers and Occupiers, plus the special interest groups, and, most importantly, those who have a significant financial interest in the laws that Congress enacts. And we can't leave out the major corporations, which now, thanks to the Supreme Court in Citizens United v. FEC in an apparent tribute to George Orwell, have joined the ranks of "we the people."

The founders had assumed that the mischief caused by these factions would be dealt with at the state and local level. But clearly this has not happened. As the industrial revolution mushroomed from the late 18th to the early 21st century, the amoral desire for the accumulation of wealth has now become the zeitgeist for our political philosophy and its power has been consolidated in Washington D.C.

How culpable are we the people in all of this? I would argue that it's not much. Our form of government makes us wholly dependent on our representatives (and appointed officials like judges to deal with the numerous and highly complex issues of the day. And the ballot box is no match for multi-million dollar political campaigns.

Our only chance for relief, it seems to me, is the constitutional amendment process. Many have been proffered over the years to help remedy some of the concerns. Thomas Jefferson, for example, proposed that we the people ratify the Constitution every 20 years and that term limits apply to the president (which was done in 1951 through the 21st Amendment) and to members of Congress, which, as yet, has not been done. Of course, any amendment that would help mitigate the power of those who hold sway in our government will surely be given short shrift and quickly buried in the graveyard of good intentions.

Meanwhile the current dilemma in Washington is getting worse. We'll have elections in November of course, but as I point out here, that exercise is unlikely to produce anything approaching the significant paradigm shift needed to improve our current state of affairs.

So here we are in early 2012 with a critically ill economic system, a failing education system, an out-of-control public debt, a laughable immigration policy, a virtually non-existent energy policy, a ridiculously complex tax code, a bloated government, huge environmental and ecological threats and an un-sustainable appetite for natural resources—all being juggled by an ineffective president and an intransigent and inept Congress.

Who do we the people see about that?

2.3   The 800-Pound Gorilla in the Room

August 26, 2012

"But with Congress, every time they make a joke it's a law, and every time they make a law it's a joke."—Will Rogers

Here we go again through the quadrennial exercise of electing a president. Every four years, we voters have to endure a mix of ad homonyms, magical thinking, mendacity, hyperbole, hypocrisy and noise—lots and lots of noise. One would think, listening to and following the campaigns that the electee would be able to act as both the legislative and judicial branches of government.

But the president, whoever he is or will be, has relatively limited powers, constitutionally speaking. Of course all presidents tend to go rogue (call it ex-constitution) from time to time. These mostly made-up, ad hoc powers can range from making the Louisiana Purchase, to suspending habeas corpus during the Civil War, to interring Americans of Japanese descent, to authorizing torture, to sending missile-laden drones to kill Americans without due process.

But with all the hoopla over the presidential election, the 800-pound gorilla in the room these days is Congress. The president can't make laws (not officially anyway) and, through the Electoral College, is only tangentially elected to office by the people. However, in setting up our ternary government, it is clear that the Founders intended Congress, specifically the House of Representatives, to do the heavy lifting and be directly accountable to the people. That's why the Constitution establishes Congress in Article 1, granting it specifically enumerated powers;

leaving the (very limited) duties of the president for Article 2 and putting the Judiciary a distant third in Article 3. We look to the president for leadership and the courts for guidance on the law, but it's really Congress that has all the power.

To me, and many others I suppose, Congress these days is conspicuously disengaged; content, apparently, to let the country run on auto-pilot, while the members spend most of their time working toward the next election and negotiating a quid pro quo or two with contributors. And the political parties expend most of their energy blaming each other for all of our woes. Unfortunately, the blame game carries on even after they are elected. Instead of acting like grownups and working diligently to help solve the nation's problems, it seems they would rather push for more polarization and animus.

In a recent Gallup poll, Congress had a 10 percent approval rating—the lowest in 35 years. But in 2002, Congress enjoyed a whopping 54 percent approval. There is good reason, in my opinion, for this fall from grace.

To start with, consider that by the end of 2012, members of the House of Representatives will have met for 109 days, while the rest of American workers will have put in 258 days. In 2011, the House was in session for 123 days, about half the number of regular workdays that year. Although they do work on the days they are not in session, it is unclear how much of that is spent tending to the people's business and how much goes into raising money for the next election.

Among the important work Congress needs to do every year is to pass a budget. The last time Congress passed a budget from the president was in April 2009; the federal government has used continuing resolutions to fund operations since then. The traditional budget process has essentially ended due to the bickering between the parties. This has created a cloud of uncer- tainty that makes planning in both the public and private sectors difficult, if not impossible. And it is decidedly unhelpful in reducing the existential angst that attends a broken economy.

There are many examples just in the last few years of the Congress failing to serve the public interest. You can probably list them yourself. Remember the debt-ceiling crisis in the summer of 2011? Among other things that inane exercise prompted Standard & Poor's to drop the nation's credit rating—a first in the 225-year history of the country.

Then there are all the machinations over the Affordable Care Act (a.k.a. Obamacare) with a reported 33 votes in the House to repeal it (at an estimated cost of $50 million to tax-payers), even while knowing that such a bill would never make it past the Senate, much less the President's veto. This is how political polarization becomes the enemy of democracy.

In terms of work product, consider that in the 2011-2012 session (through July) Congress passed 147 bills, of which 29 of them, almost 20 percent, were for the naming of Post Offices And most of the rest were maintenance items and otherwise innocuous bills.

Our standing in the world is falling as well. In the "Index of Economic Freedom" produced by the conservative Heritage Foundation and "The Wall Street Journal," the U.S. ranked 10th place in 2012, down from third place in 2002. (If you're interested, Hong Kong, now a part of communist China, ranked first)

Currently, the U.S. ranks first in the world in per capita health expenditures, but we are laggards in some common measures of health outcomes. According to a recent Reuters report:

"Americans spend twice as much as residents of other developed countries on healthcare, but get lower quality, less efficiency and have the least equitable system, according to a report released by the Commonwealth Fund. The United States ranked last when compared to six other countries - Britain, Canada, Germany, Netherlands, Australia and New Zealand."

And the advances we have made in technology, which has given us a highly competitive edge in world markets, may be more difficult in the future. Consider that, for 2010, the Organization for Economic Cooperation and Development (OECD) ranks the U.S. fourth out of 34 countries in money spent per student on secondary education, but we are 14th for reading skills, 17th for science, and 25th for mathematics.

According to sources used by Ranking America (rankingamerica.wordpress.com.), in 2009, the U.S. ranked 187th in GDP growth, 46th in civil liberties, and 20th in freedom from corruption. In 2010, we ranked 37th in upholding the law, and 17th in democracy. But we are first in incarceration rate per 100,000 residents and in anxiety disorders.

Given those issues, it's no wonder we're only 11th in the world on the Happiness Index (based on another Gallup poll). This, despite the fact that we invented the smiley face and the happy meal.

I don't know whether the disturbing trends in our economic, political, and social health is reversible or not. But while the focal point for our progress as a nation is usually placed on the president—past, present, and potentially future—our Constitutional republic puts that responsibility squarely on the elected representatives of the people. Let's see then take on the American spirit and prove themselves worthy of representing all of us, working for the people's interests rather than their own.

It seems that our Congressmen and women are, much like the voters themselves, deluded into maintaining the status quo, proceeding under the illusion that things are business as usual. No fiddlers on the roof in this crowd; no courage to break with tradition.

And on it goes. Congress' performance in the face of the many draconian problems facing the nation is appalling and inexcusable. We all know about the high unemployment rates, the trillion-dollar deficits going out as far as the eye can see, the staggering amount of federal debt, the undecipherable income tax laws, the erosion of the middle class, the decline in house-hold net worth and real wages for the vast majority of Americans, a crumbling infrastructure, and much more. Yet Congress remains intransigent; focused on the next election, concerned more about whether their party will prevail, and seemingly oblivious to the fact that the country is hanging off a cliff by its well-bitten finger-nails.

Thomas Paine, the pamphleteer and social critic during the Revolutionary War, who is often overlooked as one of our most important Founding Fathers, wrote,

"Government, even in its best state, is but a necessary evil; in its worst state, an intolerable one."

Something to think about as we slouch toward election day.

2.4   The Right to Keep From Being Shot

April 17, 2013

On April 9, CNN's Arin Burnett interviewed Senator Tom Coburn (R-Ok) regarding his stand on background checks for would-be gun buyers. The good Senator allowed as how he would support such a measure and went on to say, "91% of Americans support background checks as long as there is no record of it." (Note: the Quinnipiac University Poll that Coburn refers to makes no mention of "records."

When challenged by Ms. Burnett on that claim, Coburn barked that the Constitution says "The government doesn't have a right to know whether I bought a gun or not." Then, in typical political double-talk, he contradicts himself by adding that we should keep guns out of the hands of the mentally ill and felons. But he fails to tell us how we will know that if we don't keep records.

Further, I can't find a prohibition in the 2nd Amendment that says the mentally ill and felons can't own guns, nor is there a list of weapons that the public is forbidden to buy such as an M-1 Abrams tank or an F-22 Raptor.

In fact, such limitations on the "right" to own guns are perfectly legal. Article 1, Section 8, of the Constitution says Congress has the power, "To regulate Commerce with foreign Nations, and among the several States, and with the Indian Tribes." That means Congress can make laws regulating the manufacture, distribution, and sale of guns, just as it has and continues to do with a plethora of other goods.

Senator Coburn and government officials at all levels should go back to the Preamble of the Constitution, to the first three words – "We the people." We the people have conferred certain powers to the three branches of government on the condition that that government protect, defend and enforce certain rights and liberties of the people. If the President and the Justices of the Supreme Court and the Members of Congress are to follow the Constitution, then that means any Executive Order, Supreme Court decision, and act of Congress must fall under the rubric of "pro bono publico" – for the public good.

To say it another way, the Preamble does not begin with "We the crony capitalists," or "We the Military Industrial Complex." or "We the lobbyists, "or " We the campaign

contributors," or " We the NRA." Among other things, this means any actions of any of the branches of government that are carried out specifically for the benefit of any special interest group which works to the detriment of We the people, would be a clear violation of these officials' oath of office to protect and defend the Constitution and, thereby, a betrayal of the public trust.

All things considered then, it seems to me the only question to be resolved by Congress with regard to the Second Amendment is whether the people's right to own guns is more important than the people's right to be keep from being shot.

2.5   Time to Quit Digging

October 13, 2013

"When the people find they can vote themselves money, that will herald the end of the republic."—Benjamin Franklin

I hate to be the bearer of bad tidings, but we, meaning we the nation, have already fallen off the proverbial fiscal cliff. We are like Wiley Coyote who, standing in midair about 10 feet away from the edge of the cliff, finds out the hard way that the law of gravity is stronger than the law of suspended animation. The ears droop, the eyes sadden and down he goes, spread eagle, so that his outline in the ground below will be recognizable.

Of course, to some of you this is no surprise. Those of us who have training in or experience with economics and finance, and those of us who have been following the mischief created by the executive and legislative branches of government over the years, have witnessed the gross mismanagement of the nation's fiscal and monetary systems. And it is getting worse.

According to U.S. Debt Clock.Org, as of October 6, 2013, the unfunded obligations of the federal government for Social Security, Medicare, and prescription drugs totals 126 trillion dollars. That's trillion. And that starts with "t." And that stands for trouble, right here in, uh, every city. Seriously though, that comes out to $1.1 million per household. (An unfunded obligation is the excess of future commitments over and above future income.) But the federal government's total unfunded

obligations actually add up to something north of $200 trillion when things like veteran benefits, federal pensions, and various welfare programs are added in. In that light, our current $17+ trillion national debt is only about 8.5 percent of the total problem.

So how did this happen? I think it's because the electorate has selective hearing. Political candidates always promise to help the rich and the poor, the elderly and the sick, the managers and the workers, the soldiers and the students, the pork-barrel projects and the lobbyists. Those elected then put the promises through the sausage grinder in Congress and make them into law, or let them fall by the wayside as the case may be.

But each constituent group cares only about its particular issue and is unaware of or indifferent to the demands of the other factions. It's when all the affected groups get their own piece of the pie that the promises and the associated financial commitments start adding up. And regardless of whether promises are kept or not, office holders are almost always assured of tenure, just so they can continue to fight the good fight.

In fact, during the 2012 election, 90 percent of house members and 91 percent of senators who sought re-election won. Yet the approval rating for Congress averaged 15 percent for 2012. More interesting, however, is a Gallup poll earlier this year, which found that 62 percent of voters approved of the job their particular representative was doing, but only 35 percent could name him or her.

Clearly, we have lost the most important mechanism for keeping our representative democracy in check. And that's a real insult to our founding fathers, as well as a real danger for the health of our nation—financially and otherwise.

For 2013, Congress's approval rating is now as low as 5 percent. Yet this once respected cornerstone of our democracy is now consumed with a pathological obsession for a single issue that holds the entire nation hostage, posits an extreme political ideology, threatens our national security and turns the blame-game into an art form.

Meanwhile, the unfunded promises made by Congress over the years continue to accumulate. Yet there are ways to mitigate these financial crises, albeit with some pain for all. But that would take the will of Congress and a commitment by the members to look beyond the next election and into America's future.

Will Rogers famously said, "When you find yourself in a hole, quit digging!" But Congress keeps digging anyway. They know the average voter can't tell an unfunded obligation from a continuing resolution. Besides, when you're talking about trillions of dollars, most people don't know what that really means anyway.

There is a real possibility that, at some point, the lights will go out in the "Shining City on the Hill" and Congress will then realize it has to stop digging and start being responsible to all the people. Hopefully by then it won't be too late.

2.6   How to Save a Drowning Man

April 20, 2014

I recently recalled an old joke about how to tell a Republican from a Democrat. It goes like this: There is a drowning man 100 feet off shore. The Republican would throw the man 50 feet of rope and make him swim half way to safety. But the Democrat would throw the man 200 feet of rope so he would have more than enough to save himself.

Of course, this little joke could be expanded to include other groups. For example, the difference between Liberals and Libertarians is that the Liberal would go to a bank, borrow money, buy a boat to go out and rescue the man, then forget to repay the loan. The Libertarian would just send him some materials so he could make his own rope.

As between a Capitalist and an Environmentalist, the Capitalist would save the man, then send him a bill for doing it. The Environmentalist, having few resources, would ask others for help, but not being able to see the drowning man, the others think the Environmentalist is just making the whole thing up to get another government grant.

I could go on, but you clever devils can make up your own satirical jibes.

The point is that we tend to think of certain characteristics of a particular group and the stereotypical behavior of the group's members when we envision a particular entity. But instead of calling them groups, or parties, or organizations, or unions, or associations, I'm just calling them "tribes."

Of course, we are members of lots of different tribes, including our family, our community, our nation, our political affiliations, our religious institutions, our fellow workers, our classmates, and the list goes on.

Even so, today's tribalism is much like it was back in the Paleolithic era. Tribes are protective of their own and suspicious of outsiders. This tribal loyalty gives rise to the mistrust of others, sometimes intolerance, and even war.

Our identity, our history and our values, are all derived from our tribe.

We will fight for our tribe, conform to its beliefs; become invested in its worldview. But we are social animals and we have evolved to depend on our tribes for safety and survival. So the success of any tribe to thrive depends on cooperation and coordination—the Golden Rule.

All of these factors create an emotional investment in our tribe and we are not apt to criticize or challenge it, much less think about it. Interaction with members of other tribes is often limited by misperceptions and biases without regard for objectivity. The messenger is shot before the message is even heard. Critical thinking is checked at the door.

But this allegiance sometimes drives our behavior beyond reason, resulting in irrational acts and even immorality like racism that lets us feel that our tribe is better than theirs, religions that create zealots who fly planes into tall buildings, politicians who ferment divisiveness and the denial of evolution or other basic scientific truths when they challenge tribal beliefs, are all examples.

Tribalism is powerful and pervasive. It is an inherent part of who we are as human beings and an imperative for our survival. In fact, it is our own tribe that informs our decision- making and the choices we make in life.

Of course, we're not in the Paleolithic era any more. We've stopped hunting and gathering and learned to domesticate plants and animals. We've moved out of the caves and into three bed-room homes. We've traded our spears for nuclear bombs.

But technology has not replaced tribalism. Those funda- mental characteristics of the tribe are deeply rooted; they are in our genes. You can see that fact play out every day in your own life, and in every report from the news media.

Maybe if we got out of our bubbles, climbed out of our boxes, took a little risk, and considered what good other tribes are doing, there might be some common ground — a common cause that would help propel each tribe forward to the benefit of all tribes. Something, anything, that would help put the civil back in civilization. We shouldn't have to wait for another terrorist bombing, or a massive hurricane, or a life-threatening fire to rally in support of each other.

So the question is: how can we use the best attributes of our own tribe and join with other tribes to coordinate, to cooperate, to save the drowning man, or more importantly, to keep him away from the water in the first place?

2.7   So Long Democracy, We Knew Ye Well. R.I.P.

May 6, 2014

"Remember, democracy never lasts long. It soon wastes, exhausts, and murders itself. There is never a democracy that did not commit suicide."— John Adams

Well, it's is now official. Liberal democracy as we knew it is no more. Or, as Nietzsche might put it, democracy is dead. And how do I know this, you ask? I know because of an April 9, 2014 report by Princeton University's Martin Gilens, and Northwestern University's Benjamin Page, "Testing Theories of American Politics: Elites, Interest Groups, and Average Citizens," that tells me the majority does not rule in the United States. Well, I was shocked, shocked I tell you.

Although the authors don't specifically use the term, some reviewers have opined that the conclusions in the report seem to fit the definition of an oligarchy — a form of government in which power rests with a small number of people. However, since the Supreme Court's decision in the McCutcheon case, which struck down the aggregate limits on contributions to political candidates, I personally thought that we had gone from a representative democracy to an unrepresentative plutocracy, or even an aristocracy.

The word "democracy" is derived from the Latin "demos," which means "the people" + "kratia," which means power and rule." So, democracy simply means "people rule." On that point, Gilens and Page comment that,

"The central point that emerges from our research is that economic elites and organized groups representing business interests have substantial independent impacts on U.S. government policy,

while mass-based interest groups and average citizens have little or no independent influence."

In other words, it's tyranny of the minority.

Of course, anyone who follows politics in this country knows intuitively that our system of governance has been in trouble for several decades, and that there are a few at the top who get the mine, while the rest of us get the shaft.

The latest Gallup poll shows that Congress has a 13 percent approval rating. That's better than the all-time low 9 percent it got in November, 2013, but it's still an F minus. The founders set up a bicameral Congress to represent all the people and thus be the engine of democracy. But the evolution of the two political parties with their absurd gerrymandering and an almost obsessive appetite for the accumulation of wealth, have helped to grind the democratic process almost to a halt.

In a poll conducted by The Associated Press-NORC Center for Public Affairs Research, "The People's Agenda: America's Priorities and Outlook for 2014," Americans expressed significant concerns in the government's ability to solve the problems they see as important. The report states,

"Large majorities are only slightly confident or not at all confident that the government can make real progress on the most commonly mentioned issues, including 69 percent for health care reform, 64 percent for unemployment and jobs, 67 percent for the economy, 85 percent for the budget and national debt, 75 percent for immigration, 63 per-cent for education, 82 percent for taxes, 70 percent for foreign policy, and 74 percent for the environment and climate change. Averaging across the entire range of problems mentioned, 76 percent of Americans report low levels of confidence that the government will make real progress toward solutions to those problems."

All of this lack of confidence in our elected officials, along with the embarrassingly high disapproval rating of Congress, and yet we still reelect incumbents 90 to 95 percent of the time. The definition of insanity comes to mind—doing the same thing over and over and expecting a different result every time. Like the House of Representatives voting 60 times to repeal the Affordable Care Act knowing all the time that it will never get passed a veto.

At the end of the report, the authors offer a minor retraction, seemingly with tongue planted firmly in cheek:

"Perhaps economic elites and interest group leaders enjoy greater policy expertise than the average citizen does. Perhaps they know better which policies will benefit everyone, and perhaps they seek the common good, rather than selfish ends, when deciding which policies to support. But we tend to doubt it."

2.8   Thoughts on the Fourth of July

July 13, 2014

"History shows that great nations rise and great nations fall, but the autopsy of history is that all great nations commit suicide." —British Historian Arnold Toynbee

Another Fourth of July is behind us. The speeches are now fading memories, the patriotic music is quiet, the hot dog eating contests are over (thank god) and the fireworks displays have fizzled out.

Everybody knows (or should know) that the Fourth of July is the day of the year when we celebrate the signing of the Declaration of Independence. At the behest of a committee of five appointed by the Second Confidential Congress, Thomas Jefferson wrote the Declaration which was then adopted on July 4, 1776.

Some observe this day as the birth of our nation, but that is wrong. To be metaphorically correct that date is when the nation was conceived. In fact, as written in the document itself, the caption was "united States of America," where the "u" was not capitalized. So, as of July 4, 1776, we went from being colonies to being States. However, by the time the Articles of Confederation were approved in 1781, we had become "United." And with the Constitution of 1787, we were officially a federal republic called "the United States of America."

While standing in the killing fields of Gettysburg in November, 1863, Lincoln famously described the Declaration, saying,

"Our fathers brought forth, upon this continent, a new nation, conceived in Liberty, and dedicated to the proposition that all men are created equal."

This first of our nation's founding documents not only declared our separation from England, but much more. As Jefferson writes in the Declaration,

"The history of the present King of Great Britain [George III] is a history of repeated injuries and usurpations, all having in direct object the establishment of an absolute Tyranny over these States. To prove this, let facts be submitted to a candid world."

The Declaration goes on to list the "injuries and usurpations" — the acts, some 27 by actual count, committed by England upon what would eventually become the United States. Although some of these grievances were specific to the times in which they were written, others are more general. In fact, many of those were later adopted for our new government, including the right to a trial by jury, the prohibition of taxation without representation and putting the military under civilian control.

Those particulars, when combined with some political philosophy from the ancient Greeks, and the Renaissance and Enlightenment philosophers, including many of the founders themselves, and much of English common law as well, were incorporated first into the Articles of Confederation, and then into the Constitution and Bill of Rights.

All well and good. But the Declaration also contains one of the most troubling and debated phrases in the history our nation:

"We hold these truths to be self-evident, that all men are created equal, that they are endowed by their Creator with certain unalienable Rights, that among these are Life, Liberty and the pursuit of Happiness."

Looking back now, it was patently, if not painfully, obvious that equality and unalienable rights were not universal at that time. Women, along with African Americans, many Native Americans and those who were not property owners, were denied those most basic liberties. However, what's lost in all the noise is the very next phrase, the one that in my opinion that is the most important in the whole document:

"That to secure these rights, Governments are instituted among Men, deriving their just Powers from the consent of the governed."

That is the glittering diamond in this old parchment. Governments are to be controlled from the bottom up, by democracy, by we the people. Again, Lincoln adds clarity to this principle at Gettysburg, concluding his speech with the resolve:

"That government of the people, by the people, for the people, shall not perish from the earth."

So the underlying importance of the Declaration of Independence was not just to proclaim a separation from Great Britain, though that was certainly a critical part, it was to turn the prevailing form of governance in Europe and in the colonies on its head. No more divine rights of kings, no more monarchies, or autocracies, or oligarchies, or plutocracies or dictatorial, megalomaniacal tyrants. Ours would be a government that must acquiesce to the will of the people and the people alone.

That, then, brings up the question that should be asked every Fourth of July — is our country operating by the consent of the governed as intended, or have the governed been replaced by the elites, the lobbyists, the trade associations, the unions, the political parties, the military industrial complex, the too-big-to-fail banks, the unaccountable government bureaucracies and the self-serving politicians looking for a lucrative quid pro quo?

Unfortunately, the fact that we the people give Congress an approval rating of 8 percent, yet reelect 95 percent of the incumbents makes the answer a paradox.

Maybe the Declaration has become a dusty relic of the past: a well-intended but unworkable idea from a bunch of white men wearing powdered wigs, fluffy shirts and shoes with shiny buckles on top — a chimera if you will — beautifully written but merely rhetorical and somewhat useless today.

Think about that next Fourth of July as you wave the flag, listen to the speeches, sing the patriotic songs, eat the hot-dogs and watch the rockets' red glare.

2.9   The Debt Ceiling Conundrum

October 12, 2015

In a few short weeks, a number of Republicans in Congress will be hand-in-hand, racing à la Thelma and Louise, toward the dreaded fiscal cliff. At that time, perhaps as early as November, the federal government will have reached the so- called debt ceiling. Unless the ceiling is raised, the Treasury Department will lack sufficient funds to pay its obligations in full, which, in turn, could cause the nation, metaphorically, to drop off the fiscal cliff.

The current debt limit, set last March, is set at $18.1 trillion. We have actually reached that level, but the Treasury Department has used "extraordinary measures" to extend the time when an increase will be needed. But time has just about run out.

The federal debt is the cumulative amount of deficits that occur when spending exceeds revenues during a fiscal year. Once the debt reaches a pre-determined level — the ceiling — it must be increased so that the U.S. Treasury can pay the govern- ment's obligations. Failure to do so could result in a fiscal catastrophe affecting all Americans and financial markets around the world.

Before 1917, the president would send his treasurer up to Congress to ask for an issuance of debt (usually bonds to raise money for specific purposes. Congress would then approve the terms and the bonds would be issued. Then, in 1917, after dealing with an increasing number of bond requests, Congress created the debt ceiling with the Second Liberty Bond Act. This law allowed the Treasury to issue bonds and take on other debt without specific Congressional approval, as long as the total amount did not exceed the statutory debt ceiling.

But over the past few years, the debt ceiling has become a political football. Threats have been made by some Republicans to freeze the debt limit using the logic that doing so would further their agenda of cutting spending and reducing the size of government. For example, the GOP in Congress blocked an attempt to raise the debt ceiling in 2013, causing a government shutdown from Oct. 1 through Oct. 16 hoping to defund the Patient Protection and Affordable Care Act, also known as Obamacare.

Ironically such actions just add to the debt problem. The Government Accounting Office estimated that the delay in raising the debt ceiling in 2011 raised borrowing costs for the government by $1.3 billion. This was due mainly to a reduced credit rating by Standard & Poor's. The Bipartisan Policy Center extended the GAO's estimates and found that the delay will raise borrowing costs by $18.9 billion over 10 years.

Some have called a delay in raising the debt limit a folly. Congress has previously approved appropriations through its budgeting process, and by law, and that threatening a default on those obligations is both irresponsible and dangerous.

Some constitutional scholars have said that, in lieu of raising the debt ceiling, the president could declare an emergency and direct the treasurer to issue bonds or other debt instruments to provide the necessary funds.

But there are many problems here. First, the separation of powers prohibits the president from usurping Congress since he is constitutionally bound to "take Care that the Laws be faithfully executed," because only Congress has the power "to borrow money on the credit of the United States."

So, absent Congressional authority, the president would be in the untenable, unconstitutional and perhaps impeachable position of having to decide which bills would be paid and which would not. And as a practical matter though, nobody would buy such bonds anyway because of the likelihood of the courts declaring them illegal and worthless.

Then there is Section 4 of the 14th Amendment that says, "The validity of the public debt of the United States, authorized by law... shall not be questioned." The 14th Amendment was passed right after the Civil War. And Section 4 was added to keep the U.S. from paying any debts or other claims of the Confederate states or of slave owners.

In his article in the Oct. 7, 2013, issue of Fortune Magazine, "Why the 14th Amendment matters in the debt-ceiling crisis," Roger Parloff writes,

"The fact that Section 4 of the 14th Amendment may provide no deus ex machina from our current predicament ... does not detract from the fact that the provision exists, retains vitality, speaks directly to our situation, and ought to weigh very heavily in the minds — and on the consciences — of the House Republican faction that is now unambiguously violating its letter and spirit ... the Framers of (Section 4) did, indeed, mean to bar Congressmen from using the threat of debt-default as a coercive tool in the arsenal of everyday politics."

It is unconscionable that certain Republican members of Congress would cause a partial shutdown of government and risk the credit and threaten default on the debt of the United States as a vendetta against the current president.

Shame on them and shame on us for electing them to office.

2.10   Why Supreme Court Opinions Need a Super-Majority

February 9, 2016

"Law is reason, free from passion."—Aristotle

And then there were eight. The passing of Justice Scalia in February 2016 left the Supreme Court in something of a dilemma. There are four left leaning justices and four right leaning. Therefore, the chances of tie votes, an equal split in opinions, would become very real. Whenever that occurs, the rule of law will have been compromised; the conservative philosophy will have negated the liberal philosophy and vice versa. And the Constitution is the worse for it.

As this is written, it doesn't look like a replacement for Justice Scalia will be moving into his office any time soon. Some say it might be more than a year before a new justice becomes available once the new president is elected in November.

But even when Scalia's replacement joins the Court, there will still be a problem. If a Democrat is in the White House, then the new justice will likely be more liberal. In that event, the Court will be five to four favoring the left, just reversing the current majority. If a Republican becomes president, then the Court's majority of the right merely stays where it was before Scalia's death.

Of course, over the four-year or possibly eight-year term of the new president, other members will leave the court.

Anthony Kennedy, a Reagan appointee, is 79, Ruth Bader Ginsburg at 83 and Stephen Breyer at 77, were both appointed by Clinton. Depending on the party of the president when any of these justices leave the court, the political influence could make the court more liberal or more conservative.

It has always bothered me that a single person, a Supreme Court Justice, can swing a Supreme Court decision that, in turn, could affect 320 million people. That is the ultimate tyranny of the minority. And if the voting of the Court continues as a simple majority, that condition will continue.

My remedy for the simple majority rule is to replace it with a super-majority requirement. And I would set that super- majority at three-fourths of the members — 75 percent. After all, the Supreme Court is literally the court of last resort. And since the justices are not elected by the people and have lifetime tenure, and since they have become increasingly divided politically, it seems to me that opinions of the Court ought to have concurrence of more than a simple majority. Among other things, a super-majority would also inspire confidence that the question at hand has been closely vetted and not just political.

The notion of a super-majority was incorporated into the Constitution to be used under certain circumstances. These are actions they thought too important for a simple majority. For example, any proposed Amendments require ratification by a three-fourths majority of the states. To the extent opinions of the Court sometimes effectively amend the Constitution, I believe that critical threshold should apply to the Court as well.

In addition, a super-majority two-thirds approval of both Houses is needed to send proposed Amendments to the states for ratification, and to override a presidential veto. A two-thirds super-majority of the Senate is needed to ratify treaties and to conduct a trial following a bill of impeachment from the House. Either house can expel one of its members by a two-thirds vote.

And if the president becomes unable to discharge the powers and duties of his office, then a two-thirds vote of both Houses authorizes the Vice President to continue those powers and duties the same as an Acting President.

Appeals from district courts to federal circuit courts are usually decided by a majority of three members of the circuit court . But the majority of three is two. So, again there is a super-majority — two-thirds — concurring on the opinion. Of course, sometimes the three-judge panel may want to refer the controversy to the full court en banc. Each circuit has between six and 28 judges — and the decision is by a simple majority.

In our federal trial courts, juries are required to render unanimous verdicts in both criminal and civil cases — the ultimate super-majority! This is testament to meeting the high standard of "beyond a reasonable doubt," maybe even a "moral certainly." Those are attributes we should expect from Supreme Court opinions.

A number of states already have some variation of a super-majority rule in their courts. They include Louisiana, Nebraska, Arizona, Utah and Virginia. In 1919, the North Dakota Constitution was amended to require four out of their five justices (80 percent) to invalidate a state law; a provision that is still in effect.

This three-quarters super-majority would also help to de-politicize the court and minimize so-called "judicial activism." It may also put a little more pressure on the justices when they grant certiorari for the cases they want to decide given the level of agreement needed for a final disposition.

That is, the controversy at issue must be a clear and consequential question for the Constitutionality. (They should be doing this anyway.) And they should stop rendering "narrow" opinions! If nothing else, a super-majority would help minimize the controversy that seems to arise in a 5-4 decision.

But more importantly, I believe the change to a super-majority would restore the Court to the vision set for it by the Founders. As Alexander Hamilton wrote in Federalist No. 78:

" . . . the judiciary, from the nature of its functions, will always be the least dangerous [of the executive and legislative branches] to the political rights of the Constitution; because it will be least in a capacity to annoy or injure them. The Executive not only dispenses the honors, but holds the sword of the community. The Legislature not only commands the purse, but prescribes the rules by which the duties and rights of every citizen are to be regulated. The judiciary, on the contrary, has no influence over either the sword or the purse; no direction either of the strength or of the wealth of the society; and can take no active reso-lution whatever. It may truly be said to have neither FORCE nor WILL, but merely judgment; and must ultimately depend upon the aid of the executive arm even for the efficacy of its judgments."

This inherent weakness of the judiciary was not lost on President Andrew Jackson. When the Supreme Court ruled in favor of the Cherokee Nation (Worcester v. Georgia) by 6-1, or 83.3 percent, effectively eviscerating the "Indian Removal Act of 1830" that Jackson had fought Congress so hard to get, he supposedly barked, "They have made their decision. Now let them enforce it!"

On the other hand, President Eisenhower stepped up to his enforcement duty. In 1957, when Arkansas Governor Orval Faubus called out the national guard to keep Little Rock's school system "separate but equal," President Eisenhower dispatched the 101st Airborne Division to remind the governor of the Supreme Court's 1954 desegregation decision in Brown v. Board of Education (voting 9-0) and to disabuse him of any notions he may have of noncompliance.

Those are just a couple of cases where the super-majority has compelled compliance by the mere force of its near unanimity. Of course, the Court has issued opinions with concurrence ranging from a simple majority to a unanimous agreement. Some of the more important cases since the founding of the nation, along with the votes by the justices, were listed by "USA Today" and they include:

- Marbury v. Madison, 1803 (4-0 decision) - Established the Supreme Court's power of judicial review over Congress.
- McCulloch v. Maryland, 1819 (7-0 decision) - Established the federal government's implied powers over the states.
- Dred Scott v. Sandford, 1857 (7-2 decision) - Denied citizenship to African American slaves.
- Plessy v. Ferguson, 1896 (7-1 decision) - Upheld "separate but equal" segregation laws in states.
- Korematsu v. United States, 1944 (6-3 decision) - Upheld internment of Japanese Americans during World War II.
- Brown v. Board of Education, 1954 (9-0 decision) -Separating black and white students in public schools is unconstitutional.
- Gideon v. Wainwright, 1963 (9-0 decision) - Criminal defendants have a right to an attorney even if they cannot afford one.
- New York Times v. Sullivan, 1964 (9-0 decision) - Lawsuits based on libel or defamation must show intent or recklessness.
- Miranda v. Arizona, 1966 (5-4 decision) - Prisoners must be advised of their rights before being questioned by police.
- Loving v. Virginia, 1967 (9-0 decision) - Invalidated state laws prohibiting interracial marriage.

- Roe v. Wade, 1973 (7-2 decision) - Women have a constitutional right to an abortion during the first two trimesters
- United States v. Nixon, 1974 (8-0 decision) - President can- not use executive privilege to withhold evidence from criminal trial.
- Regents of the University of California v. Bakke, 1978 (5-4 decision) - Upheld use of race as one of many factors in college admissions.
- Bush v. Gore, 2000 (5-4 decision) - No recount of the 2000 presidential election was feasible in a reasonable time period.
- Lawrence v. Texas, 2003 (6-3 decision) - Struck down state laws that prohibited sodomy between consenting adults.
- District of Columbia v. Heller, 2008 (5-4 decision) - Citizens have a right to possess firearms at home for self-defense.

With exception of Miranda v. Arizona, the major decisions by the Warren Court of the 50s and 60s were unanimous. It's clear too that, since the Bush v. Gore decision, all but one of the major cases was decided by a simple majority 5-4. Politics, it seems, has raised its ugly head in Supreme Court deliberations over the last 40 years or so. In fact, polls show that public approval of the Supreme Court has dropped over the last 15 years; from 59 percent in 2000 to 49 percent by the end of 2015. But job approval of the Court goes to extremes between political parties. 80 percent of Republicans were happy with the court in 2000, probably because of the Court's decision that effectively made George W. Bush president. But the GOP's approval rating crashed to 18 percent in 2015, which was most likely due to the Court's opinion on gay marriage and upholding the Affordable Care Act (Obamacare.) Of course, the approval ratings by the Democrats were the mirror image of the Republicans with 42 percent in 2000, rising to 76 percent in 2015.

Now, I don't know the best way to deal with situations where the Court is unable to reach the three-fourths hurdle. I suppose it would be the same as a tie vote or a hung jury.

The issue could be sent back to the lower courts with or without requests for additional information. Where the case involves a federal statute, it could be sent to Congress for further disposition.

In consideration of the above, I'm not so naive as to think this proposal has anything more than a snowball's chance of going anywhere. But we the people are in agreement that our government is dysfunctional. So, if this idea ever becomes workable, then perhaps at least one branch of government can better perform its function.

NATIONAL SECURITY

3.1   Terms and Conditions for Government Surveillance

January 10, 2012

When you first signed up for an internet service provider, or activated new software, or become a paid member of a web- site, did you read the "terms and conditions"? Me neither. After all, the disclosure is rather long and sometimes written in legalize, so few of us really want to take the time to deal with it. We just check the "accept" box and hope for the best.

Of course, there are a number of other transactions including bank loans, credit cards, health care, airline travel, and others, where a disclosure is provided to you, by law, concerning what your rights are and how your personal information will be used. Therefore, you always have the option to walk away if you are uncomfortable with the terms. Although, as a practical matter, we rarely do.

These days, thanks to the advances in computer hacking, some of the personal data you thought would be secure can be captured, or, more accurately, stolen. A recent example being the credit card information hacked at the Target stores. But even here, there is some recourse, legally and otherwise, to mitigate the damages.

No, you just check the "approved" box without doing your due diligence. You have then granted permission to a provider to use the information you have freely given subject to the "terms and conditions" that you failed to read. Anything that happens to that data, then, is on you.

But the government argues that any of its spying activities that may include you are:

(1) due to a compelling government interest in national security, that such authorization for the spying was established by law by your elected representatives and,

(2) that you gave your consent, implicitly, as one of "we the people" who granted certain powers to the government under the Constitution and thereby agreed to be bound by them.

I thought of the foregoing in the context of government surveillance programs as conducted by the NSA, the CIA, the FBI, Homeland Security and other related agencies. Unlike commercial transactions, I was never given the opportunity to agree or disagree with the government going through my phone records or bank records or credit history, or emails, text messages, my web search history or my travel plans (electronic breadcrumbs, as they are called).

This is a somewhat important distinction because neither Google, nor Facebook, nor my bank nor my credit card providers have a police force that can come to my house and subject me to an interrogation and/or an arrest. For private commercial transactions, then, I am (and should be) safe from any intervention by the government.

Of course, the government posits that there is a compelling government interest in national security due to an existential and ongoing threat of terrorism and that a wide surveillance net is necessary to protect me and mine from danger. But for me to check the "accept" box allowing the government to spy me, I would have to forfeit my rights under the Fourth Amendment of the Constitution, which says,

> "The right of the people to be secure in their persons, houses, papers, and effects, against unreasonable searches and seizures, shall not be violated, and no warrants shall issue, but upon probable cause, supported by oath or affirmation, and particularly describing the place to be searched, and the persons or things to be seized."

The need for this amendment evolved before and during the Revolutionary War when the red coats went door to door looking for anything that would tell them who the loyalists were and who the spies were, and where Washington's troops might be, and often seize weapons and gunpowder. Fortunately for us, the founders recognized that such reckless disregard for citizens' personal property and private documents by the government was untenable and a threat to privacy and liberty.

Of particular interest here is "probable cause." By spying on all Americans, NSA is saying, in effect, all of us — you and I — are terrorists. Otherwise, our privacy is being violated.

Indeed, the author of our Constitution, James Madison, cautioned us to beware:

> "The abridgment of freedom of the people by gradual and silent encroachments by those in power would be aghast."

That said, I have not given my consent, directly or indirectly, to allow the government to spy on me. The representatives I voted for did not get elected, so I'm subject to the tyranny of the majority. Nor did I vote to ratify the Constitution or approve any of its subsequent amendments — and neither did you. I am bound only by my moral duty as a citizen to accept (or not any laws foisted upon me). Well, that and getting arrested and going to jail.

So the surveillance of U.S. citizens in the absence of probable cause or a very specific warrant, means that the government has to somehow justify a violation of both the spirit and intent of the Fourth Amendment.

On that point, one judge, U.S. District Court Judge Richard Leon, has found that the NSA meta-data program appears to violate the Fourth Amendment, saying in part,

"No court has ever recognized a special need sufficient to justify continuous, daily searches of virtually every American citizen without any particularized suspicion."

But another judge disagrees. U.S. District Judge William Pauley said that NSA's bulk collection of phone records was legal, arguing that,

"The right to be free from searches is fundamental but not absolute. Whether the fourth amendment protects bulk telephony meta-data is ultimately a question of reasonableness."

Some think this controversy will likely go to the Supreme Court. Hopefully, the Court will expand its consideration of the Fourth Amendment beyond the narrow scope of NSA's meta-data collection and into all of the government's spying operations involving American citizens.

But if the Court OK's NSA's spying activities, then you and I and all Americans will then be monitored as if we were terrorists. And all that data will be sitting out there waiting for another Edward Snowden or "Wikileaks."

With the past as predicate, I believe the Court will err on the side of the government and suspend the Fourth Amendment — throwing another of our cherished freedoms under the bus.

George Orwell is no doubt out there somewhere laughing his butt off.

3.2   No Place to Hide

June 17, 2013

"The [National Security Agency's] capability at any time could be turned around on the American people, and no American would have any privacy left, such is the capability to monitor everything: telephone conversations, telegrams, it doesn't matter. There would be no place to hide."—Senator Frank Church

Senator Church made that statement in 1975, 38 years ago. He chaired a committee that was formed to develop legislation to rein in the CIA, the FBI, the NSA and other intelligence agencies, which had long since been operating outside the bounds of the law, including the Constitution—especially the Constitution.

The Church Committee recommended, and Congress passed the "Foreign Intelligence Surveillance Act," with the operative word here being "foreign." This act also established that a court, the FISA Court, could authorize warrant-less wiretaps.

The Stanford Law Review in a February 2014 essay, "Is the Foreign Intelligence Surveillance Court Really a Rubber Stamp?" reports that, "Between 1979 and 2012—the first thirty- three years of the FISA's existence, federal agencies submit-ted 33,900 ex parte requests to the court. The judges denied eleven and granted the rest: a 99.97% approval rate.

Beginning in 2004, the FISA court started approving "national security letters" These give the FBI the power to compel disclosure of customer records held by banks, telephone companies, internet service providers, and others.

In 2006, Qwest Communications refused to cooperate with the FBI's NSL's. When the matter went to court, U.S. District Judge Anna Diggs Taylor ruled that the government's domestic eavesdropping program is unconstitutional and ordered it ended immediately. The Bush administration filed an appeal and the decision was reversed.

Recently, we have learned of a program called "PRISM." It seems that for some time now the NSA has been doing exactly what Senator Church warned against all those years ago— collecting telecom and internet information, including "audio and video chats, photographs, e-mails, and documents" on virtually all Americans—they call it "meta-data."

With these secret spying programs being outed, president Obama tried to calm fears and said, "We actually expanded some of the oversight, increased some of the safeguards. But my assessment and my team's assessment was that they help us prevent terrorist attacks." Obama went on to say that, in spite of, "the modest encroachments on the privacy that are involved, it was worth us doing."

Modest encroachments? Worth the doing? You mean by playing fast and loose with the First, Fourth, Fifth, Ninth, and 14th Amendments of the Constitution? You want to protect our liberty by, uh, suppressing our liberty? What?

Well then, some important questions to ask in all this are how well are these programs are working and are they helping us prevent terrorist attacks? And, what happened to the limitation of keeping these programs focused on "foreign intelligence" as they were intended?

After 9/11, and through this date up to today, we know of 53 planned attacks on United States soil, or on planes headed to the U.S., by Islamic Terrorists. Of these, 29 were "foiled Islamic terrorist plots" and only five resulted in fatalities, which totaled 19 people—two at the LA airport in 2002, one at a Little Rock military recruitment center in 2009, 13 at Ft. Hood, also in 2009, and three from the Boston Marathon bombings.

So, let's put this in perspective. According to an article on Washingtonpost.com in September 2013, "You're Much More Likely to be Killed by Lightning than by a Terrorist," there have been more than 400,000 people killed in motor vehicles, 119, 000 homicides with firearms, and 27,960 deaths from home fires since 9/11. In 2012 alone, there were 28 deaths by lightning strikes and none by terrorist attack.

Therefore, it would be accurate to say that there is no existential threat of a terrorist attack in the United States. And even if there were, the programs we have in place are grossly ineffi- cient at detecting and stopping such threats. Exhibit 1 is the Boston Marathon bombers. We had to rely on Russia for intelli- gence on the two brothers and even that was after the fact.

So it should be absolutely clear that the real threat of Islamic terrorism in this country is way overblown. The fear- mongers and the scare-mongers have won the day. They have facilitated hysteria and fabricated paranoia.

Seems to me the sizable commitment of resources to these counter-terrorism programs is like trying to put out a candle with a fire hose — and missing the candle!

Terrorism will never be zero, just as crime will never be zero. But given the strategy we have in place to deal with it, my concern is whether our country will devolve into a quasi- Orwellian dystopia where Big Brother is watching and listening, watching and listening . . .

As H. L. Mencken said almost 100 years ago:

"The whole aim of practical politics is to keep the populace alarmed (and hence clamorous to be led to safety) by menacing it with an end-less series of hobgoblins, all of them imaginary."

3.3   The Snowden Controversy

June 10, 2014

I felt much better informed after watching NBC's Brian Williams interview with Edward Snowden a few weeks ago. Snowden, who looked like the president of Harvard's Young Republicans Club, was articulate, self-assured and seemingly sincere in his answers. Overall, he made a cogent and well- reasoned defense of his actions.

I thought Williams asked the same questions that most of us probably would, although I felt at times like Snowden had rehearsed his answers.

Snowden explained what he did and why he did it. He gave his rationale for going to China and then Russia. He tried to give assurances that he had not been in contact with either of those country's intelligence agencies. But more importantly, Snowden gave us more details for his actions than we'd heard before.

And I was a little surprised at the scope of our spying programs, which apparently cover everything from email to cellphones to facial recognition.

A turning point for me in the interview was when Snowden revealed how badly the vast U.S. counterterrorism network had screwed up in detecting and stopping the Boston Marathon Bombing and the consequences thereof:

"If these programs aren't keeping us safe, and they are making us miss connections—vital connections—on information we already have, if we're taking resources away from traditional methods of investigation, from law enforcement operations that we know work, if we're missing things like the Boston Marathon bombings where all of these mass surveillance systems, every domestic dragnet in the world didn't reveal

guys that the Russian intelligence service told us about by name, is that really the best way to protect our country? Or are we—are we trying to throw money at a magic solution that's actually not just costing us our safety, but our rights and our way of life?"

Unfortunately, NBC reportedly cut out Snowden's comments regarding the intelligence community's gross negligence in coordinating information and connecting the available dots that might have prevented the 9/11 attack. That part didn't air, perhaps because NBC didn't want to offend the NSA and the other spy agencies, which have banked on 9/11 to justify their existence and expansion.

Of course, Snowden has stepped on some toes. Secretary of State John Kerry speaks for many in the administration and our counter-terrorism agencies. ""Edward Snowden is a coward," Kerry said to MSNBC. He told CBS, "He is a traitor." And in a CNN interview last year, Kerry claimed: "People may die as a consequence of what this man did."

Nobody has shown how Snowden's disclosures have harmed the efforts of our spy agencies, much less identify any who may have died because of it. Kerry's schoolyard name- calling is no doubt meant to deflect the obvious impact of Snowden's revelations that our spying programs are inefficient, ineffective and, as to the law, arguably indefensible. In short, Snowden has caused them embarrassment and exposed them to the light of day.

But Snowden is not alone. Other whistle-blowers came forward years ago to show how our counter-terrorism bureaucracy has repeatedly failed to make use of the data that would have kept us safe from terrorist attacks. They missed 9/11, they missed the 2009 Fort Hood shooting, and they missed the Boston Marathon bombers. It's the spy agencies who have blood on their hands, not Snowden or the other whistle-blowers.

Overshadowing all this controversy is the question of trust. We know Director of National Intelligence James Clapper lied to Congress, We know former NSA chief Gen. Keith Alexander, former NSA and CIA Director Michael Hayden and other higher-ups have lied outright or at least misrepresented what our multibillion-dollar counter-terrorism industrial complex is doing. This does not instill much trust or confidence in these officials.

In contrast, Snowden seems truthful and trustworthy, at least in comparison with those who have spoken out against him. Of course, he is a thief and he has admitted as much. As to the other accusations, they will have to be decided at trial—a fair one, I hope.

3.4   War and Humanitarianism

August 10, 2014

"Those who can make you believe absurdities, can make you commita-trocities."—Voltaire

In the immediate aftermath of World War II, the world was made painfully and shockingly aware of the atrocities, crimes against humanity and war crimes committed by the Nazis and the Japanese military.

But even before the war ended, the Allies sought to replace the ineffective League of Nations with a new organization that would provide a forum for participating nations to help maintain the peace, to share common goals and, more importantly, to focus on humanitarian needs.

Thus was born the United Nations. As stated in the UN Charter, its primary purpose is:

"to save succeeding generations from the scourge of war, which twice in our lifetime (WWI and WWII) has brought untold sorrow to man-kind."

Meanwhile, the Nuremberg trials for war crimes and crimes against humanity committed by certain Nazi military and political leaders were conducted from 1945 through 1946. Among other things, the findings from these trials culminated in the "Nuremberg Principles," which are a set of guidelines for determining what constitutes a war crime.

Next was the "Universal Declaration of Human Rights," which was adopted by the UN General Assembly in 1948.

Expanding on the UN Charter, the UDHR preamble reads, in part:

". . . disregard and contempt for Human Rights have resulted in barbarous acts which have outraged the conscience of mankind, and the advent of a world in which human beings shall enjoy freedom of speech and belief and freedom from fear and want has been proclaimed as the highest aspiration of the common people . . ."

Over the succeeding years, the Geneva Conventions regarding the treatment of combatants and non-combatants during international and civil wars were expanded, and some 17 other related treaties, pacts and agreements, including the establishment of an International Criminal Court, were adopted by most, but not all nations.

Collectively, these documents comprise what we know as the "International Humanitarian Law," sometimes referred to as the "Law of War" or the "Law of Armed Conflict." The controlling authority for the IHA is the International Committee of the Red Cross.

Of course, laws are only as good as their enforcement. Inter- national laws in particular suffer from this limitation. But laws, like morality, are swayed from time to time by the forces of religion, politics and economics. In any case, compliance by the parties in conflict is often given short shrift.

Consider, for example, Nuremberg Principle III, which states,

"The fact that a person who committed an act which constitutes a crime under international law acted as Head of State or responsible government official does not relieve him from responsibility under international law."

This principle was carried into the treaty that created the International Criminal Court in Article 27 "Irrelevance of official capacity." So, presidents George W. Bush and Barack Obama could be charged with war crimes. Of course, nobody is going to get a warrant from the ICC and haul Bush and Obama off to the Hague. Besides, the U.S. doesn't recognize the jurisdiction of the ICC anyway.

Of course, Russia's President Putin, Israel's Prime Minister Benjamin Netanyahu, North Korea's Kim Jong-Un and Syria's Bashar al-Assad among many others could be called to account for their crimes under international law.

The real problem with the law, however, is in its application to non-state actors or "unlawful combatants" — terrorists and their sponsors. Unfortunately, the ICC does not define terrorism, so it is usually treated by the affected nation as a matter of self-defense and subject to that nation's own laws.

Unfortunately, the effectiveness of International Human- itarian Law is about the same as the laws of the UN member nations themselves. That is, the rich and powerful can get away with much more than smaller nations with fewer resources.

Besides, most nations ignore international law anyway. Rather than go to court to punish offenders, they use sanctions, or blockades, or boycotts, or, as a last resort, war.

Maybe we've just come full circle since the end of World War II. Our determination to have a world of peace and make "freedom from fear and want . . . the highest aspiration of the common people" seems to have stalled.

According to Wikipedia, there were 195 wars or armed conflicts between 1875 and 1944, but 241 from 1945 to now, an increase of 24 percent. Hmmm.

Well, there's always World War III.

3.5   Searching for the Least Worst Decision

September 8, 2014

"The greatest danger of a terrorist's bomb is in the explosion of the stupidity that it provokes."—Octave Mirbeau

A few weeks ago, most of the world recoiled in shock at a video showing the decapitation of American journalist James Foley by a terrorist group that calls itself the Islamic State of Iraq and Syria, or ISIS . More recently, ISIS put out another video titled, "A Second Message to America," showing the beheading of American journalist Steven Sotloff. And they promise more in the future.

These images, along with many others, of these militants dressed in their black garb and using U.S. made arms, have had a profound effect on the West, especially here in the U.S. There are cries of outrage and demands that president Obama do whatever is necessary to eliminate ISIS forever, including putting boots on the ground, to use a worn-out phrase. But that is not a strategy. That is revenge. We would be doing what ISIS wants— sending in more Americans to kill, thereby creating a propaganda tool to lure even more recruits to their ranks.

However, there are the Chicken Little cries by some of our political leaders like Representative Mike Rogers, Chair of House Intelligence Committee, Senator Dianne Feinstein, chair of the Senate Intelligence Committee, and perpetual war mongers Sen. John McCain, and his faithful companion, Sen. Lindsey Graham. They and others claim that ISIS is coming over here to do us great harm. But others contend there are no imminent threats — no clear and present danger, not now.

But even if there were a threat to our security by these fanatics, or any other terrorist group for that matter, we are well prepared to deal with it. Consider that post-9/11, we have spent almost $4.4 trillion on security according to The Cost of War Project.

This includes the $1.4 trillion we've spent on the Iraq and Afghanistan wars. The rest of the cost includes the creation of the Department of Homeland Security with its 240,000 employees, the expansion of our 17 intelligence/spy agencies, and the care and treatment of the veterans of the two recent wars. And by the way, this doesn't include the cost of the beefed up anti-terrorist operations incurred by state and local governments since 9/11.

So, not to worry. Your government can easily protect us from terrorists even though virtually all the cost was paid for with more national debt, which, in itself, is terror of another kind.

With the homeland safely protected, the existential question now is "how will we protect American interests in the Middle East?" Our nation-building efforts have been total failures.

In his New York Times editorial, "The Revolt of the Weak," (Sept. 1st, 2014) David Brooks opines,

"There has been a norm, developed gradually over the centuries, that politics is not a totalistic spiritual enterprise. Governments try to deliver order and economic benefits to people, but they do not organize their inner spiritual lives. This is precisely the norm that ISIS and other jihadi groups are trying to destroy. If they succeed, then the Middle East will devolve into a 30 years war of faith against faith. Zealotry will be rewarded, and restraint will be punished."

Therein lies the problem. Even if we do manage to eliminate ISIS, how long will it take them to regroup and emerge later as

National Security | Page 71

ISIS 2.0. Then there is 2015, when we will have withdrawn from Afghanistan and must consider the possibility of a refreshed and determined Taliban and Al Qaeda 2.0 pouring out of Pakistan to reclaim what was theirs prior to 9/11.

At the end of the day, it's the Arab states that have the most to lose. Unless they get their respective acts together, terrorism will continue indefinitely. Libya is already a failed state, which has raised concerns by Algeria and Morocco.

Iraq may soon follow suit. And trouble is brewing in Egypt and Pakistan, with the latter being a state with nuclear bombs.

To make matters worse, hatred of the U.S. by citizens of these countries continues to grow, thereby driving more and more malcontents into the terrorist group de jour.

It's at least worth pondering whether we should take a hands-off approach and let the people in that area sort it out for themselves. Maybe then we can stop the bleeding that comes from the blowback we created in the first place, and that we seemingly refuse to acknowledge.

In any case, President Obama now finds himself in a no win double bind; all decisions are bad. So, as is usual in these situations, it's a search for the least worst decision. I'm just glad

I don't have to make it.

3.6   Torturing America's Values

December 14, 2014

"The United States is committed to the worldwide elimination of torture and we are leading this fight by example." -George W. Bush

---

Although I am loath to use "Senate" and "intelligence" in the same sentence, nonetheless, the Senate Intelligence Com- mittee released its report a few months ago on the use of torture after 9/11. Although I haven't read it, much of the report apparently reveals and confirms what was already known about our torture programs, a.k.a., "enhanced interrogation techniques," conducted by the CIA.

Committee Chairwoman Sen. Dianne Feinstein (D-Calif, in presenting the report to the Senate on December. 9, called the CIA's actions in the aftermath of 9/11:

". . . a stain on our values and on our history. The release of this 500-page summary cannot remove that stain, but it can and does say to our people and the world that America is big enough to admit when it's wrong and confident enough to learn from its mistakes."

Sen. Feinstein went on to name names, including presidents Bush and Obama, former CIA directors, top military brass and lawyers who, through some labyrinthine logic, opined that tor- ture — er — enhanced interrogation techniques, were legal.

Besides, they say they were merely following the directive in the 2001 Congressional Resolution, "Authorization for Use of Military Force Against Terrorists," which says, in pertinent part:

". . . the President is authorized to use all necessary and appropriate force against those nations, organizations, or persons he determines planned, authorized, committed, or aided the terrorist attacks that occurred on September 11, 2001 . . ."

None of this, because most it was widely known anyway, should be surprising. Nor should it be surprising that those who authorized and were directly involved in these programs, meaning those who put "a stain on our values and on our history," are not being held accountable. They argue that they were merely trying to obtain information that would either help us: (a) find those behind the 9/11 attacks or (b) head off any future attacks.

On Dec. 9, Senator John McCain, the only member of Congress who has endured torture, made a speech in support of the report. McCain said, in part,

"The truth is sometimes a hard pill to swallow. It sometimes causes us difficulties at home and abroad. It is sometimes used by our enemies in attempts to hurt us. But the American people are entitled to it, nonetheless.

"They must know when the values that define our nation are intentionally disregarded by our security policies, even those policies that are conducted in secret. They must be able to make informed judgments about whether those policies and the personnel who supported them were justified in compromising our values; whether they served a greater good; or whether, as I believe, they stained our national honor, did much harm and little practical good."

"What were the policies? What was their purpose? Did they achieve it? Did they make us safer? Less safe? Or did they make no difference? What did they gain us? What did they cost us? The American people need the answers to these questions. Yes, some things must be kept

from public disclosure to protect clandestine operations, sources and methods, but not the answers to these questions."

In 1987, the U.S. entered into a UN treaty called, "Convention Against Torture and Other Cruel, Inhuman or Degrading Treatment or Punishment." President Reagan signed it that year and in 1994, a Republican Senate ratified it. Based on the obligation in the treaty that member states establish laws consistent with the treaty's terms, Congress, by unanimous vote, adopted the War Crimes Act of 1996. This statute defines torture and related acts consistent with the Convention.

The pertinent definitions in the Torture Statute (18 U.S.C. § 2340) are:

(1) "Torture" means an act committed by a person acting under the color of law specifically intended to inflict severe physical or mental pain or suffering (other than pain or suffering incidental to lawful sanctions) upon another person within his custody or physical control;

(2) "Severe mental pain or suffering" means the prolonged mental harm caused by or resulting from

   (A) The intentional infliction or threatened infliction or severe physical pain or suffering;

   (B) The administration or application, or threatened administration or application, of mind-altering substances or other procedures calculated to disrupt profoundly the senses or the personality;

   (C) The threat of imminent death; or,

(D) The threat that another person will imminently be subjected todeath, severe physical pain or suffering, or the administration or application of mind-altering substances or other procedures calculated to disrupt profoundly the senses or personality.

However, 10 years later, the Supreme Court ruled in Hamdan v. Rumsfeld that Common Article 3 of the Geneva Conventions applied to the War on Terrorism, implying that any interrogation techniques that violated Common Article 3 constituted war crimes. The Bush administration, apparently aware that its "enhanced inter-rogation techniques" were, in effect, war crimes, scrambled to water down and to make legal, that which was illegal under the treaty. Thus came the Military Commissions Act of 2006, which amended the War Crimes Act.

Just as we were getting out of the torture business, along come the killer drones. Although accurate figures are hard to find, most sources I consulted say that there are many innocent victims — including children — of drone attacks; collateral dam- age, the government calls it.

Drone strikes in countries we are not at war with that cause numerous unintended casualties against persons who may or may not be a threat to the U.S., seem to me are as much "a stain on our values and on our history" as torture. (See Op-Ed 4.1, "A New Star Chamber?".)

Back in 2007, I wrote a letter to then House Speaker Nancy Pelosi requesting the commencement of impeachment proceedings against President Bush and Vice President Cheney, citing a number of offenses that insult our Constitution and the rule of law; i.e., "high crimes."

Here I will just paraphrase the ending of that letter as if it were directed to President Obama and other officials who continue to outrage the American conscience in their prosecution of the war against terror.

"I would just ask that you make the short trip over to Arlington National Cemetery. Standing amid the noble souls resting there, you tell them that their sacrifice, their courage, their last full measure of devotion to their county was in vain. Tell them that their oath to protect and defend the Constitution and "bear true faith and allegiance to the same" with their very lives—at the battles of Trenton and Yorktown, Lundy's Lane and New Orleans, Fredericksburg and Gettysburg, Santiago Bay and San Juan Hill, Cantigny and Saint-Mihiel, Iwo Jima and Normandy, Pork Chop Hill and Heartbreak Ridge, Dak To and Khe Sanh, Bagdad and Fallujah, Kandahar and Tora Bora—is of no consequence today. Tell them the government they fought for and died for no longer appreciates their dedication to duty and honor. Tell them you have other priorities."

3.7 Chicken Little and the War on Terrorism in America

January 2, 2016

"Where are you going?" asks Foxey Loxey. "The sky is falling and we are going to the lion to tell him about it," says Ducky Lucky. "Do you know where he lives?" asks the fox. "I don't," says Chicken Little. "I don't," says Henny Penny. "I don't," says Ducky Lucky. "I do," says Foxey Loxey. "Come with me and I can show you the way." He walks on and on until he comes to his den. "Come right in," says Foxey Loxey. They all go in, but they never, never come out again.

That famous fairy tale provides a good metaphor for the war on terrorism here in the United States. Ever since 9/11, the screech of the hawks has drowned out the voice of reason. And the hawks have been aided and abetted by the news media.

Hysteria ensured and we have become paranoid and put in fear of our lives - a Chicken Little state of mind.

But the fear mongering of terrorism is totally unjustified.

The statistics are mind-blowing. Here in the U.S., your chance of being killed by a terrorist is minimal. The WashingtonsBlog reported on June 8, 2015, that you are much more likely to be killed by brain-eating parasites, toddlers, lightning, alcoholism, food poisoning, choking on your meal, obesity, medical errors or auto-erotic asphyxiation than by terrorists.

The lowest estimate I could find claims that Americans have a one in 3.5 million chance of being killed by a terrorist. But life-insurancequotes.org.'s "Deadly Statistics" has it as high as one in 20 million. Compare those numbers to the Insurance Institute's "Odds of Death" for 2011, which shows a one in 8,826 chance of being killed in a motor vehicle accident, a one in 28,153 chance of being killed by a firearm, and a one in 670,090 chance of dying from falling off a ladder. The list goes on, but the point is that the odds of being killed by a terrorist in the United States are remote and statistically insignificant

Of course, if you follow the news, you would think, like Chicken Little, that the sky is falling. But the news media are trapped by their content imperative that, "if it bleeds, it leads." Any shooting drives them like bears to a honey pot, and the first thing they want to know is whether it's an act of terrorism. Then, too, they expend most of their time interviewing and reporting on pompous politicians who love to grandstand, and pontificate and demagogue. And they are at risk if they offend. Media owners can get miffed and the polls themselves can pick and choose the reporters they want or isolate them from infor-mation that might be embarrassing. After all, everybody wants a good table at the annual White House Correspondents' Dinner.

As if the media bias isn't bad enough, whistleblowers who would share what they know about what's going on behind the closed doors of our anti-terrorism establishment have been muf-fled by the FBI and threatened with criminal charges. Even what little does get out is given short shrift by the mainstream media.

For example, Thomas Drake, a former senior executive of the National Security Agency, exposed the government's secret spying on Americans in 2005. In November 2007, the FBI raided Drake's residence and confiscated his computers, documents, and books. Yet all ten 10 charges against him were dropped. Of course, he lost his $154,600 per year job at the NSA and his pen- sion. Telling the truth to power can be expensive.

All the irrational railing against possible terrorist threats in this country has created a meme that is hard to dismiss.

To give a little more perspective, consider that right- wing conservatives have actually caused more deaths in the U.S. since 9/11 than Muslim jihadists. Seriously. A December 15, 2015 article in The Washington Post, "San Bernardino would make 2015 the worst year for Islamist attacks in U.S. since 2001,"says the overly zealous right-wingers have 48 deaths to their credit, which includes the recent Planned Parenthood killing of three, and the Charleston Church with nine deaths. The Post also reported that the jihadists have 45 kills to their credit, including the 14 deaths in San Bernardino. Seems like we'd all be a little safer by spying on our own homegrown terrorists.

The hysteria over jihadist terrorism in this country threat- ens or at least diminishes some of our basic freedoms, including free speech, the right to privacy, the right to due process and the right to be safe from warrant-less searches. The fact that we would risk our Constitution to sweep up a few malcontents is unconscionable. Surely there are more important problems in this country that deserve our attention.

As Adolph Hitler once said,

"The best way to take control over a people and control them utterly is to take a little of their freedom at a time, to erode rights by a thousand tiny and almost imperceptible reductions. In this way, the people will not see those rights and freedoms being removed until past the point at which these changes cannot be reversed."

Beware of Foxey Loxey.

POLITICAL ISSUES

4.1   A New Star Chamber

April 16, 2012

"We have long since made clear that a state of war is not a blank check for the President when it comes to the rights of the nation's citizens." — Justice Sandra Day O'Connor in Hamdi v. Rumsfeld, 2004

Some of you might remember the 1983 motion picture "Star Chamber" starring Michael Douglas and Hal Holbrook. It is about a secret cabal of judges — a star chamber — that metes out its own brand of justice against those it determines have wrongly been set free, which is usually on a technicality. All is fine until the clandestine judges set their assassins loose on two criminals who were actually innocent of the crimes they were charged with (but guilty of other crimes nonetheless.). Michael Douglas's character leaves the group due to a flash of morality. But the Star Chamber carried on anyway.

The movie was based on a real English court that operated from the 16th century and up until 1641. The court was housed in a room in Buckingham Palace called the "Star Chamber," which was named because of the stars painted on the ceiling.

According to Wikipedia,

"The court was set up to ensure the fair enforcement of laws against prominent people, those so powerful that ordinary courts could never convict them of their crimes. Court sessions were held in secret, with no indictments, no right of appeal, no juries, and no witnesses. Evidence was presented in writing. Over time it evolved into a political weapon, a symbol of the misuse and abuse of power by the English monarchy and courts."

Over time, The Star Chamber has become a term of art. As the U.S. Supreme Court has described it:

"[The Star Chamber] was of mixed executive and judicial character, and characteristically departed from common-law traditions. For those reasons, and because it specialized in trying "'political'" offenses, the Star Chamber has for centuries symbolized disregard of basic individual rights."

In my opinion, it may be the case today that our nation, The United States of America, has established something very similar to the Star Chamber. And it has been operating for a long time. Consisting of persons at the highest level of our govern- ment, there has been a camarilla of self-appointed "judges" who make life and death decisions concerning individuals around the world, including Americans, without the benefit of due process and in violation of international law.

As to Americans being the victim of this ad hoc panel of ignoble officials, a seminal event occurred in September 2011 that shined a bright light on this issue. Sometime during that month, a missile strike from a U.S. drone killed a Muslim cleric named Anwar al-Awlaki, who was an apparent operative of al- Qaeda but more importantly an American citizen who was then hiding in Yemen. He was accused of plotting attacks against the U.S. Of course, the fact that our government can designate and then assassinate American citizens living (or hiding in other countries without the benefit of their Constitutional rights has caused some- thing of an outrage by the defenders of civil liberties.

In fact, the ACLU has filed suit to require the CIA to respond to its Freedom of Information request for details about who was involved in the decision-making, what facts were considered, what the legal justification was, etc. But the CIA, as only the CIA can, simply uses what has become known as the Glomar response, "We can neither deny or confirm . . ." It's all top-secret, don't ya know?

However in a speech at Northwestern University Law School in Chicago on March 5, 2012, Attorney General Eric Holder championed the practice, declaring that,

"Due process' and 'judicial process' are not one and the same, particularly when it comes to national security. The Constitution guarantees due process, not judicial process."

He followed this up with the incredulous statement,

"The principle of humanity requires us to use weapons that will not inflict unnecessary suffering."

Well, I'm glad we're being humane about it. No doubt al-Awlaki was a bad guy and it may be provable that he was planning to overthrow his nation of birth and provide aid and comfort to its enemies. If so, then he would be considered a traitor. The Constitution addresses treason In Article III, Section 3, and provides, among other things, that,

"No Person shall be convicted of Treason unless on the Testimony of two Witnesses to the same overt Act, or on Confession in open Court. The Congress shall have Power to declare the Punishment of Treason. . . ."

Note the use of the terms "conviction," "testimony," and "open court." Even traitors get due process.

But General Holder apparently ignored the Constitution,

choosing instead to substitute the administration's interpreta- tion of a joint resolution entitled "Authorization for Use of Mili- tary Force," passed by Congress on September 18, 2001. It reads in pertinent part:

Public Law 107-4, SEC. 2. AUTHORIZATION FOR USE OF UNITED STATES ARMED FORCES. (a) IN GENERAL.-That the President is authorized to use all necessary and appropriate force against those nations, orga- nizations, or persons he determines planned, authorized, committed, or aided the terrorist attacks that occurred on September 11, 2001, or harbored such organizations or persons, in order to prevent any future acts of international terrorism against the United States by such nations, organizations or persons.

General Holder may also be referring to the National Defense Authorization Act of 2012 (NDAA) that President Obama signed into law on December 31, 2011. This law effectively hands over control to the military to arrest, torture and even kill terrorists on American soil. It also allows the military to hold suspected terror- ists indefinitely without a trial or due process. There is a question, however, whether these provisions apply to U.S. citizens even though President Obama issued a signing statement specifically excluding them.

General Holder further opined that,

"The Constitution does not require the president to delay action until some theoretical end stage of planning, when the precise time, place, and manner of an attack become clear. [That authority is] not limited to the battlefields in Afghanistan. We are at war with a stateless enemy, prone to shifting operations from country to country."

Well, what if the ne'er-do-well Anwar al-Awlaki was hiding out in Canada? Would we send a fully armed drone up there to take him out? How about in Russia? Switzerland? OK, if a missile is too much, how about Seal Team 6? If not, then are we to further apply your "judicial process" only to selected Middle Eastern or African countries?

Moreover, General Holder's position lets us conveniently bypass our extradition treaties with other countries. The problem is that most of them, like the more civilized Canada and virtually all of Europe, deny extradition back to the U.S. if the accused may be subject to the death penalty. But, hey, who needs extradition when you've got an unmanned drone armed with guided missiles?

It seems to me that Holder predicates his theory on the notion that when American bad guys are holed up in other countries, the Constitution does not apply. Under that argument, as part of our war on crime, for example, we could go over to Sicily to hunt down and kill Americans who we are pretty sure are in the Mafia, and who we think might be planning to murder someone in the U.S.

Likewise with the war on drugs, where we could hunt down and kill Americans who are suspected of belonging to drug cartels and who may be hiding in Mexico or any number of Central and South American countries. But in prosecuting these two wars — the war on drugs and the war on organized crime — we don't do that.

In fact, the New York Times reported last December that a suspect in the February (2011) killing of a United States Immigration agent was extradited to the United States from Mexico and ordered held without bail pending trial. So, it appears that the Constitutional protections of trial by jury and due process that are afforded suspected criminals don't apply equally to the "bad guys" who receive the wrath of our military. Hmmmm.

Most of the civilized world respects the rule of law. Con- sider Israel for example. The Mossad, Israel's equivalent of the CIA, has hunted down, captured and then returned many suspected Nazi war criminals back to Israel for a trial; thus giving them their day in court and honoring due process. Even Iraq, after its "liberation" by the U.S. lead Coalition Forces, and using its shiny new constitution, gave the cranky Saddam Hussein a proper trail. And these guys were not just "planners." They were, as President Bush would say, really bad "evil-doers."

Of course, the U.S. mostly spins international law like the Common Article 3 of the Genova Conventions (which outlaws inhumane treatment and torture) to fit its own needs. And it has never recognized the International Criminal Court. Heck, we can't even figure out how to try enemy combatants in our criminal courts rather than in military tribunals. Regarding the latter point, Colin Powell has noted that, ""In eight years the military commissions have put three people on trial. Two of them served relatively short sentences and are free. One guy is in jail." And we continue to ignore the fact that even cruel dictators like Chile's Augusto Pinochet and Yugoslavia's Slobodan Miloševic were granted due process under extradition treaties.

Then there is the problem of getting bad information and killing the wrong people. Everybody knows that we legally execute some people in this country only to find out later they were innocent of their crimes. This, even after the legal system is strained to its limit in protecting due process. But there are no do-overs here.

The war on drugs and the war on organized crime are carried out by law enforcement. But with all the hysteria and existential angst after 9/11, the war on terrorism has been elevated to a status deserving of military action. We have created a vast complex of military, intelligence, and security operations aimed at terrorism. In my opinion, through the Patriot Act, and other related anti-terrorist legislation, our Constitution has become another casualty of this war.

Vengeance is slowly eroding the rule of law. We have become international vigilantes.

On the issue of staying within the Constitution and giving terrorists their rights, General Holder would do well to read the Center on Law and Security's report "Terrorist Trial Report Card, 2001-2009," which says this on page 10:

"The Department of Justice (DOJ) has indicted 828 defendants. Trials are still pending against 235 of them, leaving 593 resolved indictments for purposes of analysis. Of these 593, 523 defendants were convicted on some charge either by guilty plea or after trial, resulting in an 88.2% conviction rate. Seventy defendants were not convicted."

Some time ago, a friend asked me, "As a direct result of the Patriot Act, enhanced interrogation and warrantless wire taps, how many American lives so you think have been saved or grievous injury avoided?" My answer to him was that it would be the same number of lives that would have been saved by following the Constitution. Neither situation can be proved one way or the other. Of course, the latter protects everyone's liberty, while the former denies it.

The right to a trial by jury, due process, facing your accusers and Habeas Corpus go back 800 years to the Magna Carta. Those rights and many others have been incorporated into our Constitution. They may be inconvenient for law enforcement and the military, but they are there to protect you and me and anyone anywhere who is suspected of being a criminal (or a terrorist) but is not one until convicted by a jury.

But it's the people at the top — the generals, the CIA director, the Secretaries of State and Defense and Homeland Security, the president, and others who call the shots (pun intended.)

Hiding behind questionable interpretations of the law, they mete out their own brand of justice. They meet in secret, with no indictments, no right of appeal, no juries, and no witnesses. They are the new Star Chamber. And they can ignore the law and use unmanned, heavily armed drones to kill Americans.

4.2   From Russia With . . . Irony?

September 22, 2013

The Syrian dilemma, at least as far as chemical weapons are concerned, has seemed to resolve itself. Russian President Vladimir Putin came riding in on a white horse, shirtless of course, leaving President Obama and Secretary Kerry in a dust cloud of indecision while neatly getting the Syrian regime to turn over its stockpile of chemical weapons—which it said it doesn't have. This was a real coup for the top Russian, who gave the Obama administration a "teachable moment" in both leadership and diplomacy on the international stage. As a former KGB agent, Putin surely must have laughed out loud at the irony.

Meanwhile, we, meaning the Obama Administration, are throwing our weight around by demanding this, that, and the other thing, as negotiations proceed on how to best secure and account for these WMD's. We need everybody to know that we will keep our Tomahawk cruise missiles ready to launch on a moment's notice in the event of noncompliance.

But Mr. Putin just couldn't resist taunting us with his success in defusing the Syrian crisis. He went and wrote an op- ed piece for the New York Times. This was truly a "truth-to- power" moment. In commenting on the president's address to the nation on September 10th regarding our

"Exceptionalism" (to be the world's policeman), Putin replies, "It is extremely dangerous to encourage people to see themselves as exceptional, whatever the motivation." Of course, that phrase became the attention-getter for the media, as Putin no doubt intended.

More importantly, Putin has exposed the raw underbelly of our foreign policy — arrogant, hegemonic, shortsighted, hypocritical and imperialistic. He is just saying out loud what other nations have said quietly for decades. By our actions, these are the attributes that have infused the foreign policies of the U.S. Not democracy, not humanitarianism and not civil rights, as we would like to believe.

By any measure, we have the largest military force on the planet. According to the "Base Structure Report" from the U.S. Department of Defense, the United States is the largest operator of overseas military bases, with as many as 662 sites in 38 countries in 2010. Not surprisingly, then, military action is at or near the top of the list for dealing with international conflicts — real or not.

In the case of Syria, our Secretary of State, the nation's designated peacemaker, talks of war. Our Secretary of War, er, Defense is conspicuously absent from the debate. And General Martin E. Dempsey, Chairman of the Joint Chiefs of Staff, just looks at his shoe laces and says very little.

In another irony, if we use any kind of unilateral military action in Syria without a UN resolution to do so, that in itself would be an act or war and a violation of international law. In other words, the United States would be breaking international law to punish another country for breaking international law.

Maybe the way of getting around the legal problems is just to avoid ratifying treaties, which requires approval by two- thirds of the Senate in the first place. To that point, Wikipedia's page "List of treaties unsigned or un-ratified by the United States" shows that the U.S. has yet to ratify some 37 international treaties. They include the Convention on Discrimination against Women, the Convention on the Rights of the Child, the International Covenant on Economic, Social, and Cultural Rights, the Biological and Toxin Weapons Convention, and the Ottawa Treaty that bans Land Mines — the latter being the one Princess Diana worked so hard to get adopted.

Written between the lines of his Op-Ed piece, President Putin is reminding us that the Cold War is over, and that our dealings with the world should not be delivered on the tip of a spear. "We must stop using the language of force and return to the path of civilized diplomatic and political settlement," he says.

But our moral compass, it seems, points directly to the military industrial complex.

4.3   I Like IKE and So Should You!

November 4, 2013

"In the councils of government, we must guard against the acquisition of unwarranted influence, whether sought or unsought, by the military-industrial complex. The potential for the disastrous rise of misplaced power exists and will persist." —Excerpt from President Dwight D. Eisenhower's Farewell Speech to America on January 17, 1961.

Thus was born the phrase that has embedded itself in our lexicon—"military-industrial complex."

As Supreme Allied Commander for the European theater during World War II, Eisenhower saw war up close and personal. He knew firsthand of the massive devastation unleashed in the fight to defend freedom. And he saw too the barbarism and evil that human beings are capable of. His position as president, no doubt informed by his wartime experience, was to use mili- tary might only as an absolute last resort.

Eisenhower began his presidency in 1953. At that time the world was still recovering from the wreckage of World War II, and there was political upheaval aplenty. The newly formed state of Israel was fighting for its survival, Mao Zedong and his Chinese Communist Party had taken over China in 1949, the revolution in Algeria, which began in 1954, ultimately led to its independence from France in 1962, and to top it off, there was the Hungarian Revolution of 1956. In our own backyard, the Cuban Revolution resulted in the overthrow of Fulgencio Batista by Fidel Castro in 1959.

This was also the era of the Cold War, which was becoming warmer and warmer as the U.S. and the Soviet Union were building nuclear weapons and missiles to deliver them. The fear of communism, called the "Red Scare," was the prevailing sentiment throughout the decade. Of course, these days we might call it the "Terrorist Scare." The paranoia is the same.

Eisenhower was in an unstable and uncertain world that could, at any given time, become nothing more than a radio-active cinder. Yet, in the face of these dangers, Ike reduced the country's defense budget and re-configured the military to meet the needs of his day. According to the Department of Defense's "Green Book FY 2014," and adjusted for inflation, Ike's defense budget for 1953 was $515 billion, but when he left office in 1961, it was down to $371 billion (again, in today's dollars.) That's a reduction of almost 28%!

What's more is that the U.S. did not participate in any military (or police) action during Ike's presidency!

Today, 60 years later, we're in a different world with different treats to our national security. The policy question now is just "how much of a defense budget for the military do we really need?" The Cold War is over. There is no real existential treat from any other nation, except maybe North Korea, and the machinery of war is a whole lot different than it was in the 1950s.

Yet we have seen an explosion of activity in the military- industrial-complex since Eisenhower left office. In fact, some say we have seen the "disastrous rise of misplaced power," that he warned us about.

About 50 miles north of Reno, NV, there is an Army depot where more than 2,000 M-1 Abrams tanks sit motionless next to the Sierra Nevada Mountains. The Army says it has more than enough tanks available to meet its needs, but Congress has nonetheless authorized the acquisition of more tanks. It's likely that most of these will go to the desert as well.

In 2006, the Air Force got Congress to approve the construction of the Lockheed Martin F-35 Lightning II. This was to be the ultimate multipurpose fighter jet, replacing the F-16's and F-18's. However, the plane has repeatedly failed fight tests and pilots have expressed concerns with its safety. A GAO report last year found that the cost to buy 2,457 next generation F-35 stealth fighters reached $395.7 billion, or 42 percent more than the 2007 estimates.

Meanwhile, the Navy has its own problems. According to the Congressional Budget Office "Analysis of Navy's Fiscal Year 2013 Shipbuilding Plan," the U.S. Navy plans to acquire six "Gerald R. Ford" class "Supercarriers" in the 2013-2042 fiscal years. They will replace the older "Nimitz" class. The construc- tion cost of the first of three Ford class behemoths is $12.9 billion — the most expensive warship ever built.

But a Bloomberg.com news article on July 20, 2016, reports that "the carrier isn't ready for warfare," and "may struggle to launch and recover aircraft, mount a defense and move munitions. On-board systems for those tasks have poor or unknown reliability issues, according to a June 28 memo obtained by Bloomberg News.

The Navy's plan is to always have at least 11 "Supercarrier" groups. Russia and China have one Supercarrier each.

With the current pressure on spending, along with the cuts mandated by the "sequester," the Department Of Defense is reducing its military budget, taking it from $589 billion in 2009, to an estimated $460 billion by 2017. But the concern remains as to whether we have the right configuration for the 2010's, since we are chasing terrorists rather than fighting other nations.

Given the size of our military, it seems to me that we're using a shotgun to kill a fly. A flyswatter is much cheaper— and more effective— kind of like a drone.

I don't know if we can ever get the military-industrial- complex under control. But I believe we would do well to listen to President Eisenhower again. In his "Chance for Peace" speech in 1953, he reminded us that:

"Every gun that is made, every warship launched, every rocket fired, signifies, in the final sense, a theft from those who hunger and are not fed, those who are cold and are not clothed."

Think about that as you drive by the army depot in Nevada that has all those acres and acres of abandoned M-1 tanks glistening in the afternoon sun. That is, if tanks actually glisten.

4.4 Life, Liberty and the Pursuit of Health Care

February 24, 2014

During the 17th and 18th centuries, during a period of philosophic thought called the Enlightenment, the idea of "natural rights" was all the rage. With few exceptions, the philosophers of the day felt that human beings were born with certain immutable rights and that the protection of these rights must be a condition of the establishment of a government; e.g., an integral part of the social contract.

The most influential proponent of this thinking was John Locke. Consider this from Locke's "Second Treatise of Government" (1690):

"The state of nature has a law of nature to govern it, which obliges every one: and reason, which is that law, teaches all mankind, who will but consult it, that being all equal and independent, no one ought to harm another in his life, health, liberty, or possessions."

In writing the Declaration of Independence, Thomas Jefferson borrowed heavily from Locke, coming up with this most familiar phrase:

"We hold these truths to be self-evident, that all men are created equal, that they are endowed by their Creator with certain unalienable Rights, that among these are Life, Liberty and the pursuit of Happiness."

(Of course, the " all men" part is a little misleading since the notion of political correctness was unknown back in 1776 .)

The Declaration was actually a list of complaints against England's' George III, used to justify our separation, as Jefferson put it, from the British Empire. But, more importantly, the Declaration also set forth the political philosophy of a secular government, which was adopted by the founding fathers and became the raison d'être for our Constitution and Bill of Rights — the organic law of the United States.

The ultimate purpose of this organic law was to enable people to freely exercise certain rights with minimum interference by the government, and the protection of these rights is why, to paraphrase Jefferson, governments are instituted among men. So, what are rights? It turns out that the scope of a "right" is fairly broad. Consider this definition from a legal dictionary:

"Right 1) n. An entitlement to something, whether to concepts like justice and due process, or to ownership of property or some interest in property, real or personal. These rights include various freedoms, protection against interference with enjoyment of life and property, civil rights enjoyed by citizens such as voting and access to courts, natural rights accepted by civilized societies, human rights to protect people throughout the world from terror, torture, barbaric practices and deprivation of civil rights and profit from their labor, and such American constitutional guarantees as the right to freedoms of speech, press, religion, assembly and petition."

Some legal scholars have argued that there is a property interest in some rights, including natural rights, civil rights and human rights. As to human rights, for example, Murray F. Rothbard writes in his series on the Ethics of Liberty:

". . . there are two senses in which property rights are identical with human rights: one, that property can only accrue to humans, so that their rights to property are rights that belong to human beings; and two, that the person's rights to his own body, his personal liberty is a property right in his own person as well as a 'human right.'"

So even though rights can be considered property, they are not commodities. There is no invisible hand in the marketplace driving economic decisions pertaining to rights.

Notwithstanding U.S. Supreme Court opinions to the contrary, rights cannot be bought or sold.

Abraham Lincoln referred to Jefferson's eloquence in the Declaration four score and seven years later in Gettysburg, saying,

"Our fathers brought forth on this continent, a new nation, conceived in Liberty, and dedicated to the proposition that all men are created equal," and that, "government of the people, by the people, for the people, shall not perish from the earth."

These words, along with their nexus to the Declaration of Independence, were memorialized in the 14th Amendment in 1868, which provided for citizenship rights, privileges and immunities, due process and the equal protection of the laws.

Our government was therefore founded on the principles of assuring and protecting the natural rights and the liberty interests of we the people. These, to me, are not just limits on the government, but moral imperatives.

By extension then, our elected officials at all levels have a moral obligation, and arguably a legal one as well, to help assure that all Americans are afforded the unalienable rights of life, liberty and the pursuit of happiness, which, among many others, should include health care.

On that point, consider that in 1798, Congress passed and President John Adams signed into law, "An Act for the Relief of Sick and Disabled Seamen." The Act authorized a small deduction from the wages of seamen for the sole purpose of funding medical care for sick and disabled seamen, as well as building additional hospitals for their treatment.

Now, President Adams was not only a member of the committee that drafted the Declaration of Independence, but was also a delegate to the Constitutional Convention in 1787. Ergo, Adams was fully aware of and uniquely qualified to discern the intentions of his fellow founders regarding the people's rights and the appropriate functioning of the federal government.

In fact, according to a Washington Post article by Adam Rothman, an associate professor of history at Georgetown University, wrote:

"It [the Act for the relief of Sick and Disabled Seamen] is a good example that the post-revolutionary generation clearly thought that the national government had a role in subsidizing health care."

I think it can be argued, then, that the law providing health care to disabled seamen could be a predicate to the Patient Protection and Affordable Care Act (a.k.a. Obamacare, even though the latter was in force 212 years earlier.

To the extent that a life is lost or that liberty and the pursuit of happiness are compromised by any American due to the lack of health care, then those elected officials responsible for legislation that would ameliorate such suffering, but refuse to do so, are thereby denying the rights promised to that citizen through the establishment of our republic. Such legislators are, in effect, alienating those rights. And their allegiance to fundamental American values should be called into question under the Ninth Amendment:

"The enumeration in the Constitution, of certain rights, shall not be construed to deny or disparage others retained by the people."

In addition to life, liberty and the pursuit of happiness, and those specifically enumerated in the Bill of Rights, such "unenmerated" rights might include,

- Right to movement and travel Right to choose a mate
- Right to reproduce Right to privacy
- Right to enjoy the fruits of one's labor Right to free association
- Right to create and invent
- Right to own, develop and dispose of property

There is no way to list all the possible rights protected by the Ninth Amendment. And health care, at least as we know it today, was virtually nonexistent in the early days for the republic. It's understandable, then, that health care was not singled out as a specific right.

Today we have the U.S. Department of Health and Human Services, and almost every state has an equivalent agency. Consider that there is government-provided health care for the bad guys in our prisons.

And, under the 1986 "Emergency Medical Treatment and Active Labor Act," hospitals are required to accept and treat anyone who comes to the emergency room regardless of their ability to pay (but then the hospitals recover that "lost income" through higher charges for those who can pay).

Then there is Medicaid. If you qualify, you can get "free" health care, courtesy of the taxpayers.

Of course, health care is also provided to our active and retired military veterans and their families at low or no cost. The Veterans Administration and TRICARE provide these services. On October 1, 2013, the Department of Defense established the

"Defense Health Agency" which coordinates health care services through the various services for current and former military personnel and their families.

So, the U.S. already has a kind of socialized health care system, but in a patchwork of programs at both the federal and state levels. Internationally, the U.S. is party to Article 98 of the "Geneva Convention relative to the Treatment of Prisoners of War," which went into force on Oct. 21, 1950. It reads, in part,

"[Prisoners of war] shall be allowed, on their request, to be present at the daily medical inspections. They shall receive the attention which their state of health requires and, if necessary, shall be removed to the camp infirmary or to a hospital."

A breach of this Convention is a war crime and possibly a crime against humanity. So, if it's a crime to refuse health care to POWs, then what is it when the health care of a U.S. citizen is withheld or denied by the U.S. Government?

In my opinion, any legislation dealing with health care reform should be bifurcated; one part needs to deal with health "care" and the other with health "costs." It's really the "cost" part that is of most concern to all the stakeholders. The term "health care reform" is therefore misleading because the primary focus is on medical expenditures, as distinct from medical treatment.

Opponents of health care reform argue that health care should be run mostly by the private sector due to the efficiency and competitiveness of a free market and because, well, the government is lousy at running anything. Of course, any benefits the private sector produce as the result of competition accrues mainly to insurance, pharmaceutical, and medical equipment and supply companies. Health care providers that have one-on-one contact with patients—doctors, nurses, hospitals, clinics, therapists and rehabilitation facilities—provide services that, by their nature, do not lend themselves to market-based pricing. There is little or no competition going on between the providers and, obviously from the record, there are no incentives to provide the best possible service at the lowest possible cost. You rarely see an ad from a doctor that offers a free appendectomy if you have your gall bladder removed.

In the absence of control over health costs by the invisible hand of the free market, or by government fiat, the Health industry is having a hayday. From a November 11, 2013 article in The Huffington Post, "Why U.S. Health Care is Obscenely Expensive, In 12 Charts," Consider these statistics:

- A Nov. 11, 2013 article in The Huffington Post "Why U.S. Health Care Is Obscenely Expensive," says that at $8,508 per capita, and taking up 17.7% of GDP, the cost of health care in the U.S. is the highest in the world.
- In that same article, The Huffington Post says that the U.S ranks 46th in the world for the quality of its health care system and is positioned between Serbia and Iran.
- According to CIA's World Fact Book for 2014, the U.S. ranks 42nd in the world in average life expectancy. Japan ranks 3rd and the European Union ranks 37th.
- CIA's World Fact Book for 2014 also reports that the United States is 169th in the world for infant mortality. Poland is 168th, and Serbia is 170th.
- An August 20, 2013 report by the Kaiser Foundation, "Employer Health Benefit Survey," annual health insurance

premiums for family coverage went from $5,791 in 1999 to $16,351 by 2013, an increase of 281%. Meanwhile, the Census Bureau reported that the inflation-adjusted average household income in 1999 was $75,428, but by 2012 it was $71,274, a decrease of 5.5%.

- Bankruptcies due to medical bills increased by nearly 50 percent in a six- year period — from 46 percent in 2001 to 62 percent in 2007, says CNN in its June, 2009, report, "Medical bills prompt more than 60 percent of U.S." bankruptcies."

- From Melinda Beck's February 23, 2014 article in The Wall Street Journal, " How to Bring the Price of Health Care Into the Open," The average charge for joint-replacement surgery, ranged from $5,300 in Ada, Okla., to $223,000 in Monterey Park, Calif. Even in the same city, there were huge swings. The charge for treating an episode of heart failure was $9,000 in one hospital in Jackson, Miss., and $51,000 in another.

- Internationally, prices for drugs vary significantly. According to a 2013 report by The International Federation of Health Plans, prices for Celebrex ranged from $51 in Canada to $225, in the U.S. The price for Nexium is $23 in the Netherlands, and $215 in the United States.

- Yours truly's cost for a 90-day supply of the anti-depressant Lexapro (20 mg/day) was $680.78 on September 28, 2013 under Humana's Part D prescription plan, and $270.00 on January 15, 2014 under Express Scripts Medicare Part D plan. Both scripts were name brand only (not generic) and both were purchased at the very same pharmacy.

- And ProCon.org's article, "Should Prescription Drugs Be
  Advertised Directly to Consumers?," reports that all western nations, with the exception of New Zealand and the
  United States, have historically banned direct advertising
  of pharmaceuticals to consumers.

These are all symptomatic of a failed health care system in the
United States, both in terms of economics and the quality of service. And while I am loath to have government interfere any more
than necessary, it seems to me that some of the excesses found in
the system must be reined in. In fact, the current situation screams
for strong action by the government. It has the legal and moral obligation to do whatever is needed to assure that the unalienable right
of the people to adequate health care is protected.

This is no different, it seems to me, than the government's obligation to keep the country safe from attacks by other nations or
by terrorists. Money is no object when it comes to protecting our
freedom and liberty, nor should it be when it comes to life and the
pursuit of happiness.

So, in my view, it is way past time for the U.S. to join the rest
of the developed nations in the world and assure that uni- versal
health care is made available to all of its citizens. And it can be
done in a way that preserves the private sector's interests while
also assuring that the public's interest is the top priority.

If we do this, the sky will not fall and the nation won't devolve into a socialist state. I promise. After all, a healthy citizenry
is a happy citizenry. And happy people tend to vote for those who
helped make them so.

On that note, we should do all we can to make the Affordable Care Act the best it can be. Those who are trying to see it fail
are betraying our country's founding principles and, thereby, are
driving us further away from the moral high ground.

4.5 When "Give 'em Hell" Truman Actually Gave 'em Hell

August 8, 2015

"The Japanese began the war from the air at Pearl Harbor. They have been repaid many fold. If they do not now accept our terms they may expect a rain of ruin from the air, the like of which has never been seen on this earth."—President Harry S. Truman, excerpt from public statement, Aug. 6, 1945.

We have reached the 70th anniversary of the bombing of Hiroshima, Japan (Aug. 6, 1945) and Nagasaki, Japan (Aug. 9, 1945) with nuclear weapons; the first and last time such weapons have been used against an enemy during wartime.

Over those 70 years, the debate about whether President Truman should have authorized the use of such horrific ordnance has been almost constant. Many of the arguments center around the events themselves and the cruel and heinous impact they had on the men, women and children living in and around the drop zones. It is a condemnation of some racist, immoral, inhumane acts against tens of thousands of defenseless people.

But Truman's decision to use atomic bombs on Hiroshima and Nagasaki cannot be judged in isolation. There were a host of other existential issues that loomed large and hung, like Damocles' sword, over his head.

Japan had been defeated long before Hiroshima and Na- gasaki. She had already lost an estimated 315,000 lives from the fire bombings on Japanese cites by the U.S. and its allies. Its military industrial complex was almost totally destroyed.

Japan did sue for peace, however. The problem was that they would not agree to the unconditional surrender that Truman,

Clement Attlee (who replaced Churchill and Stalin had agreed to in the Potsdam Declaration on July 26, 1945.

After the bombing of Nagasaki on August 9, Truman released a statement for the press, which reads, in part:

"The world will note that the first atomic bomb was dropped on Hiroshima, a military base. That was because we wished in this first attack to avoid, insofar as possible, the killing of civilians. But that attack is only a warning of things to come. If Japan does not surrender, bombs will have to be dropped on her war industries and, unfortunately, thousands of civilian lives will be lost.

"Having found the bomb we have used it. We have used it against those who attacked us without warning at Pearl Harbor, against those who have starved and beaten and executed American prisoners of war, against those who have abandoned all pretense of obeying international laws of warfare. We have used it in order to shorten the agony of war, in order to save the lives of thousands and thousands of young Americans.

"We shall continue to use it until we completely destroy Japan's power to make war. Only a Japanese surrender will stop us."

One of the major problems, I think, was that the Western allies did not understand Japan's culture. To them, surrender was dishonorable and cowardly. The only acceptable alternative was to fight to the death. Drawing on this ethic, it was easy to get Kamikaze pilots to fly suicide missions. Likewise, the Air Force Association website states that:

"Millions of women, old men, and boys and girls had been trained to resist by such means as attacking with bamboo spears and strapping explosives to their bodies and throwing themselves under advancing tanks."

Even the Japanese soldiers that hid out on islands that were liberated by the Allies refused to surrender or accept that Japan had capitulated. (The last to "surrender" was Hiroo Onoda who stayed on Lubang Island in the Philippines until 1974!)

In a letter to Senator Richard Russell on August 9, Truman writes:

"For myself, I certainly regret the necessity of wiping out whole populations because of the 'pigheadedness' of the leaders of a nation and, for your information, I am not going to do it until it is absolutely necessary. My object is to save as many American lives as possible but I also have a humane feeling for the women and children in Japan."

So, given the Japanese culture at the time, plus the fact that they had an estimated two million soldiers ready to fight to the death when the invasion came, the projection at the time that one million would die if we did invade the Japanese mainland may not have been exaggerated.

In the meantime, the Soviet Union was closing in. As agreed to under the Potsdam Declaration, on August 8, two days after Hiroshima, the Soviets sent a million-man army into Japanese-occupied Manchuria. Although they lacked a navy sufficient to invade the mainland, their presence in the area still posed another threat that Truman would have to deal with un- less the war ended as soon as possible.

Meanwhile on the home front, everybody was tired of war. Nazi Germany had been defeated. Certain goods were still being rationed like gasoline and sugar. (Rationing did not end until 1946.) U.S. war bonds became harder and harder to sell. And military planners advised that it would take another six months to invade Japan and force surrender. Those issues no doubt weighed heavily on Truman.

There was also the potential fallout (no pun intended) resulting from the use of nuclear weapons to be considered. Nazi Germany had started a program in the 1930s to investigate the possibility of using nuclear fission. Even though it never made much progress, there was still the concern that they might make a bomb before we could.

On that point, J. Robert Oppenheimer, the scientific director of the Manhattan Project wrote In August 1943:

"It is possible that the Germans will have, by the end of this year, enough material accumulated to make a large number of gadgets (meaning atomic bombs) which they will release at the same time on England, Russia, and this country."

At the end of the war, the U.S. and its allies were trying to recruit the scientists working on Germany's nuclear program, but they had to complete with the Soviet Union, which was also after them. In any case, the genie was out of the bottle. The race was on. The Cold War had begun.

I believe President Truman made the right decision. We'll never know whether more lives would have been lost without using such terrible weapons. But after the bombs were dropped and we learned of the devastation, Truman's famous epithet, "give 'em hell" took on a whole new meaning.

SOCIAL ISSUES

5.1   Oskar and Huck

January 10, 2011

When Steven Spielberg was approached by NBC to broadcast his masterpiece film, "Schindler's List," he had two conditions: first, no commercial interruptions during the entire three-and-a-half hour running time; second, the movie must be uncut, with not one frame left out or altered. NBC agreed and the show aired on Feb. 23, 1997.

Even though Spielberg warned before the movie started about its disturbing content, some potential "offendees" watched anyway; and then complained. One was Senator Tom Coburn (R-OK), who issued a release saying that network television had sunk, "to an all-time low, with full-frontal nudity, violence and profanity," and should not have aired, "on a Sunday evening during a family time."

Well, Tom, we really don't care if you were offended by what scholars regard as the most accurate depiction of the Holocaust ever made. If you were titillated by the full-frontal nudity of people walking into a gas chamber, or offended by the profanity or shocked by the violence, then cover your eyes and ears and mouth. It's not about you. It's about one of the most horrific periods in history, and a man, Oskar Schindler, who, as part of that history, goes from being detached and uncaring to being consumed with grief over what he had witnessed.

Today, we have another crusader who wants to protect our sensibilities–especially those of our innocent children. Enter Auburn University's Alan Gribben, who has authored a new release of Mark Twain's classic, "The Adventures of Huckleberry Finn," and, in the doing, removed 217 uses of the "N" word from the original work. In Gribben's defense, the sanitized version was done at the behest of many teachers who wanted to have the book available for the classroom, but one that would be less offensive to parents and students, especially black students.

With all due respect to Dr. Gribben, he has destroyed the whole point of the book. Huck came to find that, contrary to the ubiquitous and hate-filled racism of the day, an escaped slave — a black man — was a real human being, worthy of respect and deserving of freedom. This is a book that exposes the ignorance of that racism and transforms Huck — much like it transformed Oskar Schindler — from a bystander into a participant doing his best to help fight man's inhumanity to man

No, removing the "N"word from "Huckleberry Finn" would be like removing the material Senator Coburn objected to from Schindler's List. The meaning would be lost. And the true suffering of the African-Americans and the Jews would soon be forgotten.

This dilemma was not lost on Huck:

"It would get all around, that Huck Finn helped a nigger to get his freedom; and if I was to ever see anybody from that town again, I'd be ready to get down and lick his boots for shame. That's just the way: a person does a low- down thing, and then he don't want to take no con-sequences of it. Thinks as long as he can hide it, it ain't no disgrace."

Disgrace indeed.

5.2 Tribalism, Pluralism and Geronimo

May 4, 2011

As workmen were attaching the plaque with Emma Lazarus's poem to the pedestal of the new Statue of Liberty — the one that reads, in part, "Give me your tired, your poor, your huddled masses yearning to breathe free" — Americans were celebrating the end of the Indian wars. The lone holdouts, led by the Chiricahua Apache Chief Geronimo with his threatening band of 16 warriors, 14 women and six children, had just been captured by General Nelson A. Miles and 5,000 of his troops.

This, notwithstanding the obvious irony that the Apaches were also tired and poor, and no doubt "yearning to breathe free."

Millions of immigrants have passed by Lady Liberty, most with the hope of achieving the American dream. But history has shown that they would rather have the dream without the "American" part. This is evidenced by the fact that neigh- borhoods with specific cultural identities populate most major cities — the African Americans, the Jews, the Italians, the Greeks, the Muslims, the Chinese, Japanese, and Koreans, not to mention the large enclaves of Hispanics, and many others.

Although there has been some integration between and among these groups, mostly in the workplace, in sports, and in schools, America's "melting pot" looks more like a salad bowl, with each ingredient retaining its own unique identity.

To this point, Harvard's Robert D. Putnam, back in the dark ages of 2000, published his comprehensive study, "Bowling Alone: The Collapse and Revival of American Community."

This was a massive study based on detailed interviews of nearly 30,000 people in 41 communities across America. In his August 5, 2007, review in the "Boston Globe," titled "The Downside of Diversity," Michael Jonas commented that Putnam's study,

". . . has found that the greater the diversity in a community, the fewer people vote and the less they volunteer, the less they give to charity and work on community projects. In the most diverse communities, neighbors trust one another about half as much as they do in the most homogeneous settings. The study . . . found that virtually all measures of civic health are lower in more diverse settings."

But clearly, here in 2011, it's obvious that Professor Putnam's study didn't go far enough. We are witness to a growing animus and the lack of civility in our political parties, between labor and management, among the haves and the have- nots, the capitalists and the socialists, the liberals and conservatives, the religionists and secularists, even the Dodgers' fans and the Giants' fans.

Dr. Putnam's findings have been borne out in numerous international studies comparing different measures of social health by country, where the United States rarely makes it into the top 10, and, too often, not even in the top 20. For example, as this is written, the 2005 World Values Survey ranked the U.S.

13th in "Net Happiness," and we were 114th out of 143 countries in the 2005 Happy Planet Index. In the Economic Freedom of the World 2010 Annual Report, "Legal Structure & Security of Property Rights" we went from 1st in 1980, to 22nd in 2008, in the rankings of 141 countries and territories.

The chief restraint to our success as a society, I think, is the ages-old institution of tribalism (see Op-Ed 2.1, "Planning Seven

Generations Ahead"). And tribal loyalty, as professor Putnam found out, gives rise to the mistrust of others, sometimes intolerance, and even war. Too many tribes sharing the commons, it seems, tends to slow the advance of civilization, as the tribal council we call the United Nations can attest.

Emma Lazarus wanted to give a warm welcome to those in flight from their respective dystopias. She forgot the importance of homogeneity and, thereby, the unintended consequences of mixing cultures and exacerbating tribalism. Geronimo would understand. And he wasn't even an immigrant.

5.3   Speaking of Broadcast Media and Free Speech

January 13, 2013

Apparently, all is well at the A&E network since its top-rated show "Duck Dynasty" is returning for a new season, and its patriarch, ZZ Top impersonator Phil Robertson, has been released from suspension.

Robertson was heavily criticized for his comments in GQ Magazine for disparaging gays, blacks and those on welfare. To say his remarks were "disparaging" is putting it mildly. Having read the article, my reaction is that the show's head "quacker" presents himself as a bigot of the first order and a socially and historically challenged ignoramus. But that's just me.

The outrage from the left was predictable — the liberal ethos had been challenged in a full-on assault.

Robertson's defense from the right, also expected, focused on his religious freedom and his right to free speech. However, no conservative fell to the level of endorsing this self-described redneck whose world view is stuck in the antebellum South.

Of course, Phil Robertson is not the only celebrity caught up in a bigoted and ignorant rant. There is Paula Deen for example, whose roots are also in the South. A restaurateur, author and host of a show on the Food Network, Deen was accused of using the "N-word" at various times and was sued by a former employee for racial and sexual discrimination.

During this controversy, one of Deen's publishers dropped her, and several advertisers for her TV show also withdrew, along with most of her endorsement contracts. The Food Network did not renew her show.

All this, notwithstanding the fact that Deen appeared on all the TV news shows apologizing profusely, often in tears. The discrimination lawsuit against her, however, was dismissed — with prejudice.

Before Deen, we had Don Imus, who was fired for calling the Rutgers women's basketball team "nappy-headed hos" during his syndicated radio show on MSNBC. His remarks were both racial and misogynistic. And he was taken to task for it—with a vengeance.

Like Howard Stern, Imus was a "shock jock." Hurling outrageous insults, being flip and making demeaning remarks at will are the stock-in-trade of shock jocks. But apparently there is a line not to be crossed.

Imus, like Paula Deen, prostrated himself before the black community with numerous apologies. But to no avail. Three weeks after his untoward remarks, Imus was fired.

The question then is why Phil Robertson is able to get a pass on his offensive, hurtful, stupid and downright cruel harangue, but Deen and Imus were not?

The answer, of course, is that speech by television and radio personalities is about money. In the case of Deen and Imus, the networks were in fear of losing sponsors and viewership.

Ironically, Robertson's equally insensitive remarks have actually attracted more advertisers for A&E. And "Duck Dynasty," already one of the most watched shows on cable TV, is predicted to get even more viewers for its new season.

With very few exceptions, I abhor censorship and am a strong defender of the First Amendment right of free speech. But free speech should be understood as speech you don't want to hear. As Daniel Gilbert, professor of psychology at Harvard University, put it,

"We live in a world in which people are censured, demoted, imprisoned, and beheaded, simply because they have opened their mouths, flapped their lips and vibrated some air. Hateful, blasphemous, prejudiced, vulgar, rude or ignorant remarks are the music of a free society, and the relentless patter of idiots is how we know we're in one."

But businesses are not constitutional governments. In commercial enterprises, the right to free speech has a monetary value. Say the wrong thing, whether on the air or off, and you risk a loss of listeners or viewers, which, in turn, means a loss of advertising revenue. Censorship, at least in the broadcast media, is an important mechanism for helping to assure financial success. Their allegiance is to political correctness, not individual freedoms.

As Voltaire supposedly once declared, "I disapprove of what you say, but I will defend to the death your right to say it." Today, of course, Voltaire would have to modify this pledge slightly. "I disapprove of what you say," he would state firmly, "therefore, you're fired — unless, of course, you're in one of the most highly rated shows on cable television."

5.4   Predicting is Hard, Especially about the Future.

April 8, 2014

The great poet and philosopher Yogi Berra once astutely observed that, "predicting is hard, especially about the future."

Well, the Intergovernmental Panel on Climate Change makes it look easy.

In its latest report, "Climate Change 2013: The Physical Science Basis," issued March 31, 2014, the IPCC says in so many words (covering 1,552 pages) that the sky is falling. No kidding. This report is predicting the end of civilization as we know it. It declares with "very high confidence" that,

". . . impacts from recent climate-related extremes, such as heatwaves, droughts, floods, cyclones, and wildfires, reveal significant vulnerability and exposure of some ecosystems and many human systems to current climate variability. Impacts of such climate-related extremes include alteration of ecosystems, disruption of food production and water supply, damage to infrastructure and settlements, mor-bidity and mortality, and consequences for mental health and human well-being."

In other words: Armageddon. And all this, says the IPCC, is our fault:

"It is extremely likely that human influence has been the dominant cause of the observed warming since the mid-20th century."

Bad humans, bad, bad.

Not surprisingly, there are some who would quarrel with the IPCC over its conclusions. One of them is an organization that calls itself the Nongovernmental International Panel on Climate

Change, which is a part of The Heartland Institute, a libertarian think tank. The NIPCC also released a report on March 31, this one titled "Climate Change Reconsidered II: Biological Impacts." The NIPCC report says:

"No unambiguous evidence exists of dangerous interference in the global climate caused by human-related CO2 emissions. In particular, the cryosphere (ice and glaciers) is not melting at an enhanced rate; sea-level rise is not accelerating; and no systematic changes have been documented in evaporation or rainfall or in the magnitude or intensity of extreme meteorological events. Any human global climate signal is so small as to be nearly indiscernible against the background variability of the natural climate system."

According to the NIPCC, then, the IPCC got it all wrong and carbon dioxide is actually good for us. That's music to the ears of global warming deniers.

However, if you're going to believe the NIPCC, you should be aware that much of the data provided by its contributors — about 30 of them — was not peer-reviewed and that many were even paid for their input. Annex V of the IPCC report lists about 700 contributors, who were paid nothing. Also, the NIPCC is sponsored by a libertarian organization, while the IPCC is sponsored by the United Nations.

Well, I'm certainly no expert on climate change, but I do like charts and graphs. The IPCC report definitely takes the prize for charts and graphs. Therefore, given the dire consequences of the IPCC predictions, I am cautiously pessimistic about the future.

Of course, this controversy, if there is one, is great fodder for politicians. The liberals believe it is highly likely that a Category 5 hurricane will eventually take out New York City. The conservatives, though, are willing to take that bet.

Whatever you believe about climate change, global warming, changes in greenhouse gas emissions and the like, all of it is trumped by a variation of chaos theory known as the butterfly effect. The butterfly effect is this: "A small change at one place in a deterministic nonlinear system can result in large differences to a later state."

The common hypothetical illustration, and the way the effect got its name, is to say that the beating of the wings of a butterfly in Japan could, when combined with other weather events over time, produce a tornado in Kansas."

And that, of course, is how Dorothy ended up in the Land of Oz.

In the end, it's just like what Will Rogers, borrowing from Mark Twain, famously said, "If you don't like the weather in (pick a location), just wait five minutes.

5.5 When Politically Correct is not Politically Correct

February 24, 2015

A phenomenon popping up on college campuses around the country these days is something called "trigger warnings." Apparently used first on some feminist, self-help and social activism blogs, they were associated with rape, sexual violence, and mental illness. The idea was to warn victims about the material so as not to "trigger" any associated post-traumatic stress or related trauma or other upset.

But now, trigger warnings used on college course descriptions and assigned materials have been expanded to cover other issues, including racism, classism, sexism, heterosexism, ableism, colonialism, religious persecution, violence, suicide, bullying and more. All of which is manna from heaven for the Politically Correct Police.

Speaking of heaven, take the bible for instance. A Trigger Warning for that tome might say: "Readers are advised that this book contains graphic descriptions of atrocities, violence, torture, rape, child abuse, cruelty, misogyny, barbarism, murder, infanticide, genocide, and crimes against humanity." Well, there goes Sunday school class.

Fortunately, many college administrators and faculty have called trigger warnings absurd and anathema to the purposes of higher education and its attendant academic freedom.

In fact, the American Association of University Professors has issued a position statement on them, which reads, in part:

"Trigger warnings suggest that classrooms should offer protection and comfort rather than an intellectually challenging education. They reduce

students to vulnerable victims rather than full participants in the intellectual process of education. The effect is to stifle thought on the part of both teachers and students who fear to raise questions that might make others 'uncomfortable.'"

But trigger warnings can easily morph into censorship and the editing of material deemed objectionable, and that's an even more serious problem.

For example, a few years ago, Auburn University's Alan Gribben, authored a new release of Mark Twain's classic, "The Adventures of Huckleberry Finn," for use in public schools and, in the doing, removed 217 uses of the "N" word from the original work. This sanitized version was done at the behest of many teachers who wanted to have the book available for the classroom, but one that would be less offensive to parents and students, especially black students.

But the edited version destroyed the whole point of the book. Huck was a racist, but he came to find that, contrary to the ubiquitous and hate-filled racism of the day, an escaped slave, a black man, was a real human being, worthy of respect and deserving of freedom. This is a book that exposes the igno- rance of that racism and transforms Huck from a bystander into a participant doing his best to help fight man's inhumanity to man.

No. Remove the N-word from "Huckleberry Finn" and the meaning would be lost. The true suffering of the African-Americans would be minimized. Besides which, this book is almost unanimously regarded as a masterpiece of American literature, including by African-American authors. And you don't mess with masterpieces. (See Op-Ed 5.1)

To the extent the champions of trigger warnings are members of the PC Police, they may have gone a bridge too far. A number of speakers and others who were to appear on campus for various functions have been uninvited because they might make some students "uncomfortable." Such universities' objections include former Secretary of State Condoleezza Rice at Rutgers, women's rights activist Ayaan Hirsi Ali at Brandeis, Dustin Lance Black, the Oscar-winning screenwriter of "Milk," and an LGBT activist at Pasadena City College and conservative political pundit George Will at Scripps College, among others.

So, what we have here is no doubt a well-intended but somewhat naive effort by the PC Police to protect the sensitivities of those college students who have gone through some kind of traumatic experience. Of course, if these "victims" were not in college, then they would have to encounter the real world where they would be confronted almost daily with numerous threats to their psyche—none of which would be preceded by trigger warnings.

It seems to me those affected students would find the classroom a much safer place where any perceived threats can be put in context and thereby transformed into a learning experience.

Political correctness, then, when it operates to interfere with a person's ability to function independently in the existential world, or to diminish the quality of education, is, in my opinion, and by the law of irony, not politically correct.

5.6   About the Death Penalty

April 12, 2015

On April 29, 2015, the U.S. Supreme Court will hear arguments in the case of Glossip v. Gross. At issue is whether the "three drug protocol" that Oklahoma intends to use for executions in death penalty cases will not cause pain and suffering in violation of the Eighth Amendment, which prohibits "cruel and unusual punishment."

Back in September, 2014, Oklahoma's execution of inmate Clayton Lockett was reported as "botched." Lockett lived for 43 minutes after being administered the first drug, then had a heart attack and died. But since death was the whole point of the exercise, maybe "botched" is the wrong description. Anyway, the state has concocted a new lethal cocktail that it proposes would "fix" the problem. But Richard H. Glossip and other death row inmates in Oklahoma's state prison filed suit challenging the new protocol.

It seems that the European manufacturers of some of the drugs used in the lethal cocktail refuse to sell to the U.S. because we have capital punishment.

Absent a workable, painless, and apparently fast- acting drug protocol for lethal injections, the 32 states that still have the death penalty are looking for alternatives. Utah, for example, recently authorized the use of firing squads

The Court is not going to address the constitutionality of the death penalty in this case. That decision is implicit in their agreement to hear it in the first place — the death penalty is constitutional. It's the means of carrying it out that's the problem.

So, our most senior jurists will turn in their black robes for the white lab coats of pharmacologists.

There are those who point to capital punishment in the U.S. as being immoral and out of step with the rest of the civilized world, and that we are in the company of Middle Eastern and African states. In fact, Japan is the only other developed country with the death penalty. Most all of Europe and even Russia have eliminated it.

My own view is that the death penalty be used only in extreme cases. Consider the case of Anders Breivik, a 32-year- old Norwegian right-wing extremist, who, back in 2011, killed 69 students at a youth camp and injured at least 110 others. He was sentenced to a whopping 21 years of "preventive detention" in prison.

And then we also have the shooting of Rep. Gabby Giffords (D-AZ) in Tucson, which also happened in 2011. Jared Lee Loughner shot her in the head then turned the gun on others in the crowd killing six people, including a 12 year old girl, and wounding 13 others. Loughner, a paranoid schizophrenic, was planning the attack on Giffords for some time according to his notes that investigators found and presented at trial.

He pled guilty to 19 of the 49 counts against him and is serving life in the psych ward of a federal prison in Springfield, MO. The plea agreement took away the death penalty.

I would have Loughner put down along with Breivik. I don't like making the perpetrator of a capital crime a victim, mental incapacity or not. We don't cage a rabid dog and wait for him to die — we call Atticus Finch to shoot him on the spot.

I would only use the death sentence in cases where the evidence is overwhelming, as it was in the cases cited above, with numerous eyewitnesses who are all consistent in their testimony, and forensics that are unimpeachable.

There is no doubt that we have executed many innocent people. As of this date, the Innocence Project, which Barry Scheck and Peter Neufeld founded in 1992, and mostly using DNA evidence, has led to the freeing of 325 wrongfully convicted people, including 18 on death row [as of 2015]. The real problem with the death penalty is that there are no do- overs.

For those who were indeed guilty of capital murder, the issue of human rights is often brought up as a bar to the death penalty. But do the human rights of a murderer outweigh the hu- man rights he denied to his victims? Here I emphasize the plural of victim. The death penalty in my world would apply only to serial killers and mass murderers, and even then only when the evidence is virtually absolute. Such an approach would also comply with the Supreme Court's mandate that punishment is made "proportionate" to the crime.

In the case of capital murder, it's the state that must stand in to represent the victims who died at the hands of a murderer. Their human rights were ended in a flash. Their potential contributions to society will never be realized.

Incarceration merely allows the incarcerated to have three hots and a cot, medical care, TV, and a library, all at taxpayers' expense until they die, unless released early.

So, when the killer is strapped to the gurney and readied for the needle, his executioners need to tell him that shortly he will be joining his victims and that they would like to have a little chat with him.

Update: The Supreme Court ruled in Glossip v. Gross that executions carried out by Oklahoma's three-drug protocol did not constitute cruel and unusual punishment under the Eighth Amendment to the U. S. Constitution.

5.7 About Marriage – Gay or Straight

September 16, 2015

The Kim Davis affair, involving the county clerk who refused to sign marriage licenses for gay couples, has called attention to the sometimes overlooked wall of separation between religion and the state that our constitution demands.

The Supreme Court just recently discovered in Obergefell v. Hodges that the 14th Amendment, adopted in 1868 that included the phrase "equal protection of the laws," provides, among many other things, a constitutional right for same-sex couples to be married.

As an elected official, Davis took an oath of office to uphold and defend the constitution. The Supreme Court, for better or worse, is the voice of the constitution. Therefore, when Davis refused to issue marriage licenses to gays, acting, as she said "under God's authority." she violated her oath of office

A federal court ordered her to do her duty under the law, but she refused and was subsequently jailed for contempt of court. She is now back at work, still refusing to sign marriage licenses for gay couples. In fact, she has altered the license form itself, which calls into question whether any marriage licenses from Rowan County Kentucky on the revised form are even legal.

This is a real life example of why the founders did not want religion to play a part in government. The separation of these two institutions is set forth in the first 10 words of the First Amendment, "Congress shall make no law respecting an establishment of religion," and is called the "Establishment Clause."

But this prohibition also means that the government cannot support one religion over another or provide funding for or allow the use of government facilities for religious activities.

The Establishment Clause is followed immediately by the "Free Exercise Clause," which says, "or prohibiting the free exercise thereof." It essentially means the government can't interfere with religious beliefs as long as such beliefs cause no harm. This freedom to exercise religion, then, as with other freedoms, carries with it the idea of using it responsibly. Free speech, for example, is free unless it becomes slander or libel. As someone, probably famous, once said, "Freedom without responsibility is anarchy."

The founders recognized that religions with their various beliefs and covenants are often in conflict with each other and with the state. They also knew that such conflicts sometimes lead to violence and the loss of liberty. Having been witness to those problems in Europe, they sought refuge in America and eventually decided on a secular government as a means of neutralizing any religious influence.

And secular governments have the added advantage whereby the rule of law is derived from a single source, the constitution, and that all citizens, religious or not, share the same freedoms, the same rights, and have the same responsibilities.

So, we are a secular constitutional republic. In selecting our representatives, the founders specifically intended to make clear that there is no religious bias. To that end, language was included in Article VI of the constitution, which reads, ". . . no religious test shall ever be required as a qualification to any office or public Trust under the United States."

When it comes to Davis, then, it should be abundantly clear that she cited the wrong authority in denying marriage licenses to gay couples. As an elected official, she should know better. Of course, she is entitled to express her grievances up to and including a little civil disobedience, but only as a private citizen, not as an officer of the state

After five weeks of the Constitutional Convention in the hot summer of 1787, Benjamin Franklin noted that little progress was being made, that there was a stark division and some animus between and among the attendees, and that maybe a little guidance from above might help.

Dr. Franklin then entered a motion stating, "that henceforth prayers imploring the assistance of Heaven, and its blessings on our deliberations, be held in this Assembly every morning before we proceed to business, and that one or more of the clergy of the city be requested to officiate in that service.

Roger Sherman, representing Connecticut, seconded the motion. Discussion followed and concerns were raised about having the clergy attend the highly "secret" sessions, that that might send a signal about the difficulties they were having in getting the job done and thereby risk some states calling back their representatives. Ben Franklin's motion was defeated.

So it is interesting to note that the establishment of one of the most revered governing and organic laws ever conceived in the history of civilization was completed with much hope, but not a single prayer.

5.8   Pro Life or Pro Birth?

August 30, 2015

One of the most emotionally charged controversies of our time is that of abortion. It involves legal, religious, political, social, biological, and moral aspects, most of which center around the concept of life during the gestation period.

As to legalities, the controversy over abortion entered the public discourse in 1972, with the Supreme Court decision in Roe v. Wade. Justice Blackmun, writing for the 7-2 majority in that case, concluded that,

"Though the State cannot override that right [of privacy], it has legiti-mate interests in protecting both the pregnant woman's health and the potentiality of human life, each of which interests grows and reaches a "compelling" point at various stages of the woman's approach to term."

Those who disagreed with that ruling came to be known as "pro-life," while those who agreed became "pro-choice."

With few exceptions, polls over the past 20 years show that these groups have been almost evenly divided. Results from the most recent Gallop poll (May 6-10, 2015) showed that 50 percent of respondents were pro-choice and 44 percent were pro-life on the question of abortion. In that same poll, 51 percent of pro-lifers indicated that abortion should be legal only in certain circum-stances, while 29 percent of all U.S. adults said that abor-tion should be permitted in all circumstances and 19 percent who said abortion should be illegal in all cases.

Notwithstanding the polling results, most observers believe Republicans are overwhelmingly pro-life and that liberals are pro-choice. But the term "pro-life" may be a misnomer in the context of abortion. Consider this from Sister Joan Chittister, O.S.B. — a prolific author and outspoken critic of Catholic doctrine — addressing Republican lawmakers:

"I do not believe that just because you're opposed to abortion, that that makes you pro-life. In fact, I think in many cases, your morality is deeply lacking if all you want is a child born but not a child fed, not a child educated, not a child housed.

And why would I think that you don't? Because you don't want any tax money to go there. That's not pro-life. That's pro-birth. We need a much broader conversation on what the morality of pro-life is."

At the Iowa State Fair a few weeks ago, CNN reporter Dana Bash asked former Arkansas Governor and Republican presidential nominee Mike Huckabee, about his position on abortion. Not surprisingly, it is unequivocal. Huckabee opposes abortion even in cases of rape because "we can't discount a human life."

When asked about the 10-year old girl in Paraguay who was raped by her stepfather and denied an abortion by the state, Huckabee said that case is "horrible," but it doesn't justify taking the life of an innocent child. "I just come down on the side that life is precious, every life has worth and value," he said.

Well, not "every life." Huckabee also thinks capital punishment is "a necessary part of our criminal justice system." As Governor, he oversaw 16 executions in his state — the most of any governor before him. So, Huckabee and his ilk have a problem. They are paradoxically both pro-life and pro-death at the same time.

However, as Sister Chittister suggests, pro-lifers are not so much pro-life as they are pro-birth. Their interest in the welfare of the child stops when it draws its first breath. If the argument that life begins at conception is true, then it follows that life does not end at birth. Pro-life implies a humanitarian concern from cradle to grave.

To qualify as a pro-lifer, or at least be consistent, it seems to me such a person should also be anti-capital punishment, anti-armed conflict, and anti-women's privacy rights. Likewise, a pro-lifer should be pro-stringent gun control, pro-universal health care, and pro-expanded family welfare programs. To that point, Christopher Hale, executive director for Catholics in Alliance for the Common Good, wrote in a January 22, 2015, article in Time Magazine called "Pro-Life Is More Than Being Pro-Birth,"

"To be truly pro-life, we cannot simply support a child's right to be born, but also the right of the mother to expect substantial support from her community and from her government. We can't be pro-life and anti-woman. It doesn't work. And we can't be pro-life and anti-government. It doesn't work.

If today's anti-abortion movement transforms into tomorrow's pro-life movement, it can transcend the ideological divisions that plague our nation and proclaim a simple truth that can bind our people—especially the young—together: that everyone deserves a life, a family, and a future. But to do so, this pro-life generation must protect every person's right to live, not just be born."

To which I say, amen.

5.9   Marriage Licenses and the Wall of Separation

July 26, 2015

> *"There is nothing nobler or more admirable than when two people who see eye to eye keep house as man and wife, confounding their enemies and delighting their friends."—Homer*

Rumor has it that right after the Supreme Court issued its ruling on gay marriage, Justice Antonin Scalia went outside the Supreme Court building and met with Bobby Jindal, Ted Cruz and Mike Huckabee to see if the four of them could burn the building down.

This exasperated quartet is certainly not alone in feeling that the Court has committed a grievous error that threatens the traditional institution of marriage between a man and a woman. But this outrage mostly comes from religionists, especially those who are fundamentalists.

Take Christians, for instance. For most of the last 2,000 years, marriage for women was not exactly an equitable arrangement. In fact, marriage for the fairer sex was only one step above slavery. Consider Ephesians 5:22-24 (NIV):

> *"Wives, submit yourselves to your own husbands as you do to the Lord. For the husband is the head of the wife as Christ is the head of the church, his body, of which he is the Savior. Now as the church submits to Christ, so also wives should submit to their husbands in everything."*

This gave rise to a bride's wedding vow where she promises to "honor and obey" her husband. Although over the last few years, thanks to the feminist movement, that pledge has mostly been removed from the bride's vows.

And take note of the quote at the beginning of this piece that's attributed to Homer. He uses the phrase "man and wife" as if it were "man and horse." So, some 2,800 years ago, women were commonly regarded as unequal to men.

The driving principle of the Abrahamic religions, then as now, centered on the importance and power of patriarchy. Females are given their father's surname at birth and take on their husband's surname upon marriage. Unlike their sisters in more "primitive" cultures, such as Native Americans, wives were denied their own unique identity.

Marriage is also a property transaction. In the days of yore, it usually involved a dowry of some kind. The bride-to-be's parents would give a couple of goats and maybe a few chickens to the husband-to-be. In some cultures, the reverse is true; the groom pays off the bride's parents with a few silver coins or livestock. These days, the dowry is typically an expensive— usually diamond—ring that the groom gives the bride at the wedding ceremony (and then has to pay for it over the next 10 years). And as if that wasn't enough, the bride's father is asked to "give his daughter away," which just affirms the fact that he has transferred the wife-to-be to her husband so that she then becomes his property and takes on his name.

Of course, the conditions for marriage have changed over the years. Our little foursome of would-be arsonists should remember that interracial marriage was verboten until the Supreme Court struck down anti-miscegenation laws in 1967, in Loving v. Virginia.

They should also keep in mind that there are no laws preventing child molesters, wife beaters or rapists from getting married, or even remarried. If morality is an issue, then those caterers serving weddings who refuse to make pizza and wed- ding cakes for gay weddings should also check the criminal records of the husbands-to-be in heterosexual weddings. The county clerks who refuse to issue marriage licenses to gay cou- ples should do likewise. (See Op-Ed 5.7) It could be that their moral indignation is merely a mask for their homophobia, or perhaps they are un-comfortable with their own sexuality.

Over the years, the gay community has managed to over-come its flamboyant stereotype and disappear into the crowds of just regular folk. As for marriage, studies have shown that gay couples tend to have more stable relationships and are even better parents than their opposite-sex counterparts.

In 2010, a study from the University of California-San Fran-cisco entitled, "U.S. National Longitudinal Lesbian Family Study: Psychological Adjustment of 17-Year-Old Adolescents," the conclusion was:

"The 17-year-old daughters and sons of lesbian mothers were rated sig-nificantly higher in social, school/academic, and total competence and significantly lower in social problems, rule-breaking, aggressive, and externalizing problem behavior than their age-matched counter-parts."

Churches should not have problem in performing same-sex marriages. Jesus' second commandment (Matt.19:17-19) compels them to "love your neighbor as yourself" and Luke 6:31 requires them to follow the golden rule.

Another complication for the Catholic Church is that gay marriages (for men only) may have been acceptable in the Dark Ages. Yale historian John Boswell, in his 1994 book, "Same-Sex Unions in Pre-Modern Europe," claims to have uncovered man-uscripts that depict gay marriage ceremonies from the eighth to the 13th centuries. But gay marriages were stopped when church leaders decided marriage was only for procreation. (It's important to note here that Boswell's work has been called into question because of his bias as gay man.)

The Pledge of Allegiance ends with the phrase, "liberty and justice for all." It does not say "liberty and justice for some." Gays are full-fledged citizens who pay taxes, vote and make a contribution to the nation. They are entitled to the very same rights and privileges as non-gay citizens.

Maybe Scalia, Jindal, Cruz, Huckabee and their ilk should think about that before they burn the place down.

5.10   The Conversation About Race

July 11, 2016

In the wake of the Dallas shootings on July 7, and the Baton Rouge shootings on July 17, 2016, police, politicians, and pundits have urged the nation to have a conversation about race. I'm not sure how much a conversation would help, but to the extent there is one, I believe it should include at least some of these discussion points:

(1) Although the "Black Lives Matter" leaders have tried to clarify the meaning of that phrase, it remains ambiguous. Many whites see it as meaning blacks are being victimized by police. But there are an estimated 765,000 uniformed law enforcement officers in the U.S., and there are no doubt more than a handful of bad actors among them. The actions of a few should not be an indictment of the many.

(2) Through June 2016, The Washington Post's "police- shootings 2016 database" reports that police have killed 76 people, of which 362 were white and 188 were black. And according to the U.S. Bureau of Justice Statistics, from 1980 to 2008, 84 percent of white homicide victims were killed by white offenders and 93 percent of black homicide victims were killed by black offenders. This may be an issue that is being overlooked with all of the attention of the police officer involved shootings

(3) The USBJS also reports that in 2008, the homicide victimization rate for blacks (19.6 homicides per 100,000) was six times higher than the rate for whites (3.3 homicides 100,000) And the offending rate for blacks (24.7 offenders per 100,000) was seven times higher than the rate for whites (3.4 offenders per 100,000).

(4) Police officers know these statistics and are therefore justifiably more apprehensive when patrolling densely populated back areas in urban centers. They get cussed out, have rocks thrown at them and, at least in one case, have been bombed with nasty diapers from the rooftops. But in spite of all this, the vast majority of these officers are loyal to their oaths and serve and protect those neighborhoods.

(5) Most cops respond appropriately to potentially dangerous situations and follow their training even though the public, including blacks, may see it as too harsh. And even though there is more to do, most law enforcement agencies have made and continue to make significant efforts to expand training and to better vet applicants. Offenders should be subject to our justice system, however imperfect it is, to sort out. Otherwise, there is mob rule.

(6) In the subconscious of many African-Americans is the ugliness of 350 years of oppression, pain, humiliation, and loss of freedom—250 years of slavery and 100 years of Jim Crow. Those memes are hard wired into their souls. It's easy to understand, then, that when some blacks see a uniformed law enforcement officer, they may subconsciously see a slave owner or a KKK member with a hanging noose or a whip.

(7) There is white privilege. As a white man I can drive or walk down the street with no fear of a cop stopping me. I can go shopping without a store clerk giving me the evil eye. I can apply for a job or a bank loan without feeling conspicuous and apprehensive. I have almost total freedom to do as I please as long as I don't break the law and not be

questioned because of my race. Whites can only intellec-
tualize what it must be like to be a person of color; never
actually having the experience themselves.

(8) The constitutional right of protest does not allow for the
use of violence. The protests in Dallas over the killings of
black men by white cops in Baton Rouge and Minnesota is
a good model. Five white officers gave their lives to protect
those rights. In fact, according to an article in theatlantic.
com on July 9, 2016, "excessive force complaints against the
[Dallas Police] department dropped by 64 per-cent over a
five-year period. Arrests are decreasing by the thousands
each year. "The protests in Baton Rouge and Minnesota,
on the other hand, were not so peaceful and several arrests
were made. In those situations, the police came decked out
in military style uniforms with military weapons and riot
gear. The predicable result is that tensions rose and violence ensued. Trust is essential — on both sides of the line.

(9) There is resentment by many whites toward the black community. They see blacks getting aid for housing, education
and welfare as reverse discrimination. And they see the
deficiencies in the black community as being caused by the
blacks themselves. This is institutional racism.

(10) Then there is the understanding of the idea of equality.
That term is understood to mean equality under the law.
But equality in any context is impossible. A more appropriate term is "fairness." Everyone wants to be treated fairly.
And it is grossly unfair to be treated differently because of
skin color. The result is to create animus, resentment or a
distrust between the races and a retreat into tribalism.

Overarching any discussion on race is the common goal of improving communication to minimize hate and fear. That, in turn, will maximize trust and freedom for all. And implicit in such an objective is the need for responsibility. It would be well for us to remember the old aphorism:

"Freedom without responsibility is anarchy."

About the Author

Herb Van Fleet is a retired financial consultant and resides in Tulsa, Oklahoma. He has had no formal training as a writer except in what few writing courses he took in college many, many years ago.

After his wife passed away in 2003, Mr. Van Fleet interest in writing increased substantially. See the Preface herein for a more specific background that ultimately lead to the publication of this book.

In addition to writing op-eds, Mr. Van Fleet has created two blogs. The first created in 2010, is called, "The Absurdity Index," which offers many essays on a variety of subjects, as well as some of his op-eds. (See https://theabsurdityindex.com/)

His second blog, established in 2011, is "The Humanist Challenge," providing and expanding his view on Humanism. (See https://thehumanistchallenge.wordpress.com/)

Included in this blog, is his five-part series called "The Myth of Universal Human Rights."

He is a member of Academia.edu, which published his paper titled, "You Can Only Get Something From Nothing If Nothing Is Something." The essay, which originally appeared in The Absurdity Index, presents his thesis that there can be no uncaused cause. (See https://www.academia.edu/)

Mr. Van Fleet is also a member of the National Society of Newspaper Columnists.